VARANASI
Myths and Scientific Studies

VARANASI
Myths and Scientific Studies

Proceedings of an Interdisciplinary Workshop

Edited by
Vidula Jayaswal

Aryan Books International
New Delhi

Varanasi: Myths and Scientific Studies

ISBN: 978-81-7305-450-1

Published in **2013** by

Aryan Books International

Pooja Apartments, 4B, Ansari Road, New Delhi-110 002 (India)
Tel.: 23287589, 23255799; Fax: 91-11-23270385
E-mail: aryanbooks@gmail.com
www.aryanbooks.co.in

Computer Typeset and Printed in India at
ABI Prints & Publishing Co., New Delhi.

Editor's Note

It is for quite some years, that the focus of research of some of us, at the Banaras Hindu University, has been Varanasi, which enjoys reputation of being one of the oldest living cities of the world. Recent archaeological findings, for instance, take the antiquity of this city contemporary to the Later Vedic period (about 1800 BCE). While the geological and the remote sensing studies have demarcated palaeo-channels and ancient waterbodies of the region, which are still older in time, and have governed the successive human settlements. While exchanging notes, we reached the conscientious that an interdisciplinary study of Varanasi is imperative for unfolding facets of the multi-layered format of this cultural centre of our country. A joint investigative programme, at small scale, was also initiated at Ramnagar, which was of mutual benefit. The inferences drawn in this venture directed us towards their similarities with the event narrated in some of the popular folklore and mythological stories. The possibility for examining the myths through scientific studies appeared a challenging, but useful line of investigation.

The story of '*Ganga-avatarana* in Varanasi' is one such story which caught our attention. According to this story, which is told by *Kevata* (boat-men), while giving boatride to tourists, ... "Ganga was not flowing here (Varanasi) in remote past. Anand-kanan was situated here, which was the abode of Lord Siva and his concert Parvati". It is further, elaborated that... 'in order to help men of Varanasi, the Lord blessed them by directing the river to flow from this very region'. This story, which is also recorded in the ancient texts, like the *Kashi-khandah,* suggests that there was a time when the river Ganga was not flowing where it flows today. Recently conducted archaeo-geological investigations in Varanasi region appear to corroborate it. For, not only was there a time when the river was non-existent in this region, but, there had been geological events in the remote past, which framed the river Ganga to flow where it flows now. The enquiry which needs to be addressed, therefore, is whether the mythology of *Ganga-avatarana* is a remembrance of a very old geological incident? Or whether the two are absolutely unconnected with each other? If the geological event was at the base of the *Ganga-avatarana* mythology, then the other enquiry would be, how did this happening was converted into a myth or folk tale? In fact, all the facets, such as 'nature, process of formulation, moderation, elaboration, and even at times distortions' of myths need to be understood, before a meaningful study could be designed.

One realises that myths have deep roots in our society, and appear to sprout over the fertile culture canvas of the past. As a result, the beliefs and socio-cultural messages which are inherent in these, are mostly interwoven in our cultural behaviour. It is also obvious that through these stories, are conveyed social and cultural values, as well as scientific messages to the masses. Content and mode of narration and adaptability of myths, thus could be a promising line to be explored for understanding the roots of our culture. But, the question is whether there had been some scientific reason behind the prevalence of a belief, which has come to us since time immemorial? Also, is it possible to dwell upon the utility of this mine of culture information by the aid of scientific methods?

The core content of a myth is usually in the form of a narrative event which, may or may not, had happened, but are narrated as an important event of the remote past. The former situation brings it close to historical happenings. A critical scrutiny of myths with a view to separating them from the other narratives, may be possible when questions like, "what is a Myth? How is it different from a historical event? How does one ascertain that the origin of a myth is based on a factual happening? Through which process actual events get converted into myths", are addressed. Discourses by senior Indologists on these issues were deemed necessary. Application of scientific methods for the study was another major thrust of this venture. Thus, scientists' views on the proposed theme were of equal significance.

A brainstorming workshop was, therefore, organized by me and Prof. Rajiva Raman, on November 02, 2010, under the auspices of the Banaras Hindu University. Aimed at exploring the possibilities of designing a multidisciplinary research programme on Myths and Scientific Studies, eminent Indologists, like Dr. Kapila Vatsyayan, Prof. Kamlesh Datta Tripathi and Prof. Nawang Samten, and eminent scientists, Prof. P. Krishna, Prof. T.V. Ramakrishnan, Prof. S.C. Lakhotia, were invited. 'Our archaeological, geological and satellite imagery studies of Varanasi region', by Profs. Vidula Jayaswal, K.N. Prudhvi Raju and U.S. Shukla, and 'the comparable deductions from some select mythological narrations', by Dr. Meera Sharma and Ms. Prachi V. Sontakke, were the case studies which formed part of the theme of this academic meet.

It is to my satisfaction that the proposed session was felt to be a success by all the participants. And of course, it was very rewarding for us, as we were keen to receive directions and suggestions from the leading scholars and scientists on the proposed theme. Needless to mention that besides being par excellence in their respective fields, the above-mentioned eminent Indologists and scientists, have deep understanding of Indian culture in general and Indian thoughts in particular. I feel particularly blessed when at the suggestion of Dr. Vatsyayan, the proceedings of this workshop could be finalized, with encouraging response of all the contributors of this volume. I feel privileged to express my gratitude to each one of them.

The audio recording of the meeting was arranged by Profs. Sisir Basu and K.N. Prudhvi Raju, which helped the participants to finalize the scripts for this volume. I profusely thank them for this help.

I shall be failing in my duty if I do not mention the help and support received from Prof. B.D. Singh, the Rector and the Chairperson of the Task Force of the University, who not only suggested organization of this brainstorming meeting, but was also a constant source for obtaining administrative and financial support of the university. Moreover, his presence in person at the workshop, and presidential comments were of immense value.

Vidula Jayaswal

Contents

CASE STUDIES

OBSERVATIONS

Keynote Address

Kapila Vatsyayan

Distinguished scholars and scientists present here, and specially Prof. B.D. Singh and Dr. Vidula Jayaswal.

Allow me at the outset to thank Dr. Vidula Jayaswal for having conceived this conference on 'Myths and Scientific Studies'. She has given us a concept note which clearly lays out the parameters of our discourse. With her usual sense of precision she has drawn attention to the exploration of the subject in the context of the place of Varanasi and its environs and the contours and the movement of the river Ganga. Pertinently, she has drawn attention to the characteristics of the narrative method of myth and how it may reflect a natural phenomenon in historical time. The importance of the myth lies in its transcending specific chronological or historical time. Its value lies in the fact that this narration may be a most useful tool for undertaking scientific studies, be it in the field of geology or zoology or archaeology. We are in Varanasi. Appropriately, therefore, Vidula Jayaswal has drawn attention to the need for co-relating data from literary sources with recent geological and geomorphic studies. I have no doubt that this is going to be a most enriching dialogue.

I look forward to Dr. Jayaswal's own presentation in regard to the coherence between the narrations in the Jatakas and the archaeological sites on which she has worked so assiduously. These studies will no doubt allow us to reflect deeply on the great need for making bridges between disciplines. While some valuable work has been done in these fields in many departments, the BHU is ideally equipped to carry on such interdisciplinary and multidisciplinary studies, because it is in this university that there are the intellectual resources from diverse disciplines who can come together. I say these words in my capacity as a former student and as someone who has known the intellectual giants of the university.

The plan of this seminar includes two very important presentations from scientists—one from Prof. P. Krishna and the other from Prof. T.V. Ramakrishnan. Both these will bring up the question of whether myths have a scientific basis and whether myths can be subjected to analysis by the application of scientific methods.

As will be obvious from the above, juxtaposing of myths and science raises many, many questions at multiple levels. These include first and foremost interrogation of certain fundamental categories. Also inherent in the formulation is the question of whether myth and science are antagonistic to each other or can there be a meeting ground or can one illuminate certain aspects of the other. I know very little about the vast body of 'mythology' not only of this country but of several cultures and civilizations and even less about 'science'. Dr. Vidula Jayaswal has graciously invited me to give this initial keynote address and I am somewhat diffident and hesitant.

The words 'Myth' and 'Science' seem simple, very simple, but once you begin to address the question, its multilayered complexities come to the fore.

Let me begin from the beginning and let me again situate myself in Varanasi. The moment we begin to speak about myth and science, we have to address the question of 'Language'. Here, specially in Varanasi, can we really find an equivalent or a cognate for 'myth' in Sanskrit? I have tried to look at several encyclopaedias and dictionaries including Monier Williams and Macdonald, etc. What do I find? Myth there is called equivalent to *pauranic,* but if one translates *'pauranic'* into English, it does not become an equivalent of 'myth'! *Pauranic* is a category which may subsume 'myth' but is certainly not equal to myth. *Pauranic* is a much larger concept or category which refers to a particular genre in the Indian literary or intellectual traditions. *Pauranic* and *Ithihas* are two specific but inter-connected categories. *Pauranic* may refer to time or different orders of time, but its value lies in its potential for transcending historical time.

The English word 'Myth' comes from the Greek word *mythos* and carries with it a formidable load of definitions, interpretations and discourses over a period of many centuries. This extends from Plato to Aristotle, to the body of myths which has come down over a long period.

Briefly, one should refer to the historiography of discourse on myth in Europe. Whatever the differences were between the positions taken by Plato and Aristotle, there were distinct viewpoints—the role of imagination was stressed by one group and that of reason by the other. This is a history which we should keep in mind. Greek myths dominated the Western or the European mind for centuries. Each time these myths acquired a new meaning on contemporaneity. Prometheus of Greek tragedy is not Prometheus of Shelley, and yet the two are connected. There are some myths which become signifiers of cultures spread over a large geographical area. The myths may or may not refer to a natural phenomena or a historical event. But they do penetrate into the cultural psyche.

Attitudes towards myths and the phenomenal world undergo a dramatic change with the European Renaissance. Momentous changes take place in the perception during the Renaissance, when the new philosophy of humanism with man in the centre of the universe was promulgated. It was here that controversies began between the domains of myths and those of science. We must always remember that these discussions on science have to be situated in the European milieu, because it was the separation of science from the Church which represented religion.

To return to the discourse on myth in the West, one has to now gallop a few centuries to draw attention to Darwin and others who subscribed to a linear movement from the 'primitive' to the 'civilized'. This is a complex history of both rationalism and evolutionism. However, it is well to remember that these evolutionists or the Darwinian approach put Nature-Man in a scale of ascendancies, and no wonder that Man-Nature relationship was fractured. Wherever life and meaning was attributed to the natural world—water, vegetation, trees—it was considered to be primitive. One may mention the names of Gordon Childe, James Frazer and E.B. Taylor.

James Frazer saw myths as a misinterpretation of magical rituals, which were themselves based on a mistaken idea of natural law. He contended that man realizes that nature does follow natural laws, but now he discovers their true nature through science. He said, science makes myth obsolete: man progresses 'from magic through religion to science'.

It was only in the 20th century with the rise of Psychology with Sigmund Freud (1856–1939) on the one hand and Carl Jung (1873–1961), on the other, to be followed by those who would be considered as cultural historians or psycho-cultural historians and interpreters of myth, that we arrive at a stage when there is a vibrant discussion on universal myths—myths of the individual, myths of the collective consciousness, myths in relation to historical events, but transcending those events, local myths which emerge out of the social structures, e.g. work of Claude Lévi-Strauss, etc.

The list is long and impressive. Mircea Eliade, Joseph Campbell, and others have written extensively on the very broad and complex canvas of myths in different parts of the world. They have tried to identify certain myths as universal, cutting across different cultures. This viewpoint has been both accepted and also interrogated. The question is whether myth is context-specific or context-free.

In his appendix to *Myths, Dreams and Mysteries*, and in *The Myth of the Eternal Return*, Mircea Eliade attributed modern man's anxieties to his rejection of myths and the sense of the sacred. Joseph Campbell believed that there were two different orders of mythology: myths 'that are metaphorical of spiritual potentiality in the human being' and myths 'that have to do with specific societies'.

This is not the occasion to go into this literature. However, one must take cognizance of the polarities of views on the subject of myth, both within the ancient past as also in the modern world. One group considers myth as an essential cultural phenomenon related to the faculty of imagination and non-discursive thought. The other dismisses it as fiction and of no value. But I think no conference can ignore the discussions that have taken place in the 20th century, and even in the modern discourse one among the dimensions of the discourse has been on how myth considers a phenomenon, a natural phenomenon, and expresses that in a body of narrations, which becomes meaningful, to illuminate each other.

The word 'Science', simple as it may seem, is equally problematic. The word draws its roots from the Latin word 'scissors', which means division, reduction. As I have said elsewhere, the word 'Science' in the English language can be traced back to the Greek word 'Schizein', which has a Sanskrit cognate *chhinatti*, meaning to split. The Latin roots of the words 'scissors' and 'science' are the same. In short, all these refer to splitting, cutting, breaking and therefore analysing.

On the other hand, there is another aspect to science, and that is its relationship to mathematics, theory and experimentation. This leads to view the two domains of Myth and Science in their aspects of autonomy and distinctiveness, and yet, the time is opportune for a meaningful dialogue.

It is not for me at this stage to anticipate the richness of the discussions which will take place, except to highlight the fact that largely, as I said in the beginning, there has been a polarity between the discipline of the humanities and the discipline of science in the academia. At this stage I would only like to commend Dr. Vidula Jayaswal for having taken this brilliant initiative for a dialogue in a field which may herald not only a dialogue in the environs of Varanasi and the rich body of scholars with *Pauranic* source relating to Varanasi and Ganga but will extend further to other studies which may well bring about a new theoretical model for the study of river systems, archaeological sites and, most of all, myths which are a condensation of the Indian view on reality. All the Ganga myths refer to (a) the ecology, (b) the relationship of the primal elements with each other, and (c) capturing certain contours of river systems or forests and couching them in a language which would be indicative of specific and yet transcending the specificity of time and space.

The seminar will come to posit the myths in the vast *Pauranic* literature and their relevance for studying the geological and zoological aspects. The narratives of the Jatakas will be helpful in locating sites *in situ*.

The relationship of myth and science thus begins to make a meaning of how Indian myths, specially myths of ecology, collapse into Indian iconography. Why, for example, does the Ganga sit on the *jatas* of Shiva icon? Why does Ganga ride the *makara*? Why does Yamuna ride the *kurma*?

This is yet another field of exploration both by the botanists and zoologists as also art historians.

I leave it at this as my introductory remarks. I look forward to hearing all the papers of the contributors and the discussions.

Thank you...

Presidential Remarks

Brahma Deo Singh

It gives me immense pleasure to welcome you all to this one-day interdisciplinary workshop on Myths and Scientific Studies organized by the Banaras Hindu University. At the very outset, I would like to congratulate the organizers, Prof. Vidula Jayaswal and Prof. Rajiva Raman, for providing this very special and welcome opportunity to us for interacting with the eminent Indologists of the country—respected Dr. Kapila Vatsyayan, Prof. K.D. Tripathi, Prof. Nawang Samten, and leading scientists—Dr. Padmanabhan Krishna, Prof. T.V. Ramakrishnan, Prof. Subhash Chandra Lakhotia. On behalf of the university, I welcome this galaxy of wisdom, and all of you, the seekers of knowledge, to this academic meet.

This workshop is a part of the ongoing process, recently initiated by the Banaras Hindu University, to promote and raise the level of research, particularly interdisciplinary research, on this campus. It is well established that through multidisciplinary studies the horizon of research of each subject expands considerably, and also new directions and significant results can be obtained. In the large campus of this university, research and teaching are carried out by over 130 departments. Besides, there are a number of centres, which are involved in conducting very specialized research programmes, including teaching. It is difficult for so many units to keep track of the academic activities of each other. The university, therefore, created a Task Force, which is lead by Prof. Rajiva Raman. I have also participated in the deliberations of this committee. But, as I am senior in age, my colleagues regard me the Chairperson of this Task Force. I value this feeling as a reflection of Indian custom, but would like to record my appreciation for the efforts of the Chairperson Prof. R. Raman.

The Task Force, after considering the ongoing Research Programmes in the university, has identified twelve interdisciplinary areas. These are the subjects or research areas in which we have achieved excellence, or the subjects which we want to develop through our future research programmes. For most of us, for instance, I am a bio-technologist, Banaras Hindu University is known for its Science Faculty, Institutes of Engineering and Technology and Medical Sciences. Sometimes one also includes Faculty of Ayurveda and Institute of Agricultural Sciences. We also take it for granted that good research is being conducted only in these disciplines. But, due to the efforts of the Task Force, this incorrect and misleading view was brought to light, and it was realized that though the researches conducted in science are important, the value of the university lies in the disciplines which are involved in the study and preservation of our Cultural Heritage. As per the vision of our founder Pandit Madan Mohan Malaviya, the Indological studies and subjects related to Indian Cultural Heritage have developed as specialized areas of study in this university. Organized within four major faculties, these subjects are very active in conducting research, creative art and teaching. It is the responsibility of the university to strengthen these faculties further. It is for this reason that the Task Force has identified 'Indian Cultural Heritage' as a very important interdisciplinary thrust area. Vidulaji was requested to take initiative to organize this event, in which experts from different disciplines could participate and give us some new directions for conducting studies on ancient Indian heritage.

It is hoped that both the scientists and the scholars of traditional knowledge and disciplines will be benefited by this interactive forum. The proposed deliberations of this workshop will acquaint and inspire scientists to understand the intricacies of our culture and traditions. Such an exposure may give new outlook to a seasoned scientist, who, in true scientific temper, is used to a set pattern of designing and conducting research. On the other hand, the disciplines dealing with Indology and Heritage studies may imbibe scientific temper, which is imperative for placing the findings on firmer grounds, but is often missing in the traditional methods.

After hearing Dr. Kapilaji, I hesitate talking on the theme of this workshop. But, as part of the responsibility assigned to me, I would say a few words, with all humility. Pauranic or mythological stories are a mystic subject for me, because I know little, but have lots of imagination about these. To me, it appears that formulation of Pauranic or mythological stories is based on certain aims and needs of humans. These stories, for example, are a good way to communicate conventions, thoughts, morals, ethics to general masses. It appears that through mythology, society is directed to think and act in accordance with the inherent norms and our deep-rooted cultural traditions. Another aim, which could be fulfilled through these stories, could be the continuity of traditional thoughts on polity and legal issues. These stories transmit almost all the thoughts and conventions of our culture to the next generation. A child in India grows up listening to these stories, and unconsciously absorbs our cultural tradition. Pauranic stories are rich sources for historical studies. Kapilaji has shown through the mythology of *Ganga-avataraṇa* that some of our Pauranic stories also convey symbolic messages on important socio-cultural issues like preservation of environment.

One of the relevant questions to be asked, therefore, is whether there are scientific messages and information hidden in our mythological stories? I suspect there are many. In one of the discussions, some time back, I was told that in the text by perhaps Kanvadi there is one *śloka* (verse), which describes a formula to prepare a substance (*padārtha*). I was also told that the salt or sodium chloride grating, which is used in radars, melts under humid conditions. As a result, the utility of gratings of sodium chloride is of short span, and these have to be changed frequently. I was also informed that the substance which had been described in the above-mentioned ancient text is much better for radar grating than sodium chloride. Experiments were being carried out in some research laboratory to reproduce it. But what is the outcome of the experimentation is not known to me.

The question is, whether the text by Kanvadi is the only text which has such a formula, or there are other ancient texts like this one? We would only know this when all these texts are examined in detail for finding scientific information. It is therefore expected that, when experts from different disciplines will debate with the scholars of mythological and Pauranic studies, we would acquaint ourselves with the relevant information, thoughts and messages of Indian wisdom, and find their utility for the benefit of the society.

I am confident that due to the efforts of all the participants—senior scholars, scientists, and young researchers, students of science and Indology of Malaviyaji's *tapo-bhūmi* will be inspired to undertake researches, which are useful to the mankind.

Success of any academic meeting can be weighed in terms of the eagerness for the publication of its deliberations. It is a matter of great satisfaction that with the inspiration of honourable Kapilaji, and the painstaking efforts of the participants, it is possible to publish the deliberations of this workshop.

On behalf of the university, I offer appreciation to all the participants of the workshop on 'Myths and Scientific Studies', and the contributors of its proceedings. I sincerely thank Vidulaji for taking responsibility for editing and seeing this monograph through the press.

List of Contributors

K.D. Tripathi
Emeritus Professor, Banaras Hindu University, Varanasi, and Advisor, Indira Gandhi National Centre for the Arts, Varanasi Chapter.

Kapila Vatsyayan
Chairperson, Asia Project, India International Centre, New Delhi and Member of Rajya Sabha.

P. Krishna
Krishnamurti Foundation India, Rajghat Fort, Varanasi 221 001.

T.V. Ramakrishnan
Emeritus Professor, Banaras Hindu University, Varanasi, and Distinguished Associate, Centre for Condensed Matter Theory, I.I. Sc., Bangalore.

Viney Jain
Advisor, International School of Jain Studies, New Delhi.

Vidula Jayaswal
Professor, Department of Ancient Indian History, Culture and Archaeology, Banaras Hindu University, Varanasi.

Prachi Virag Sontakke
Assistant Professor, Ancient Indian History, Culture and Archaeology, Arya Mahila P.G. College, Varanasi.

U.K. Shukla
Professor, Centre of Advanced Study in Geology, Banaras Hindu University, Varanasi.

Meera Sharma
Post Doctoral Scholar, Ancient Indian History, Culture and Archaeology, Banaras Hindu University, Varanasi.

K.N. Prudhvi Raju
Professor, Department of Geography, Banaras Hindu University, Varanasi.

Manish Kumar Pandey
Senior Research Fellow, Dapartment of Geography, Banaras Hindu University, Varanasi.

Gautam Chatterjee
Adjunct Faculty, Department of Journalism and Mass Communication, Banaras Hindu University, and President, Abhinavagupta Academy, Varanasi.

S.C. Lakhotia
Professor Emeritus, Department of Zoology, Banaras Hindu University, Varanasi.

Views of Indologists and Scientists

1

Vedic Myths and Mythology

K. D. Tripathi

After having heard Kapilaji, I do not find any need to speak and especially on myths, mythologies and culture. The way she started with the holistic view of the world and the thought as it has been formulated in the concept of Banaras Hindu University by great founder Malaviyaji, it is natural that the deeper questions about Mythology and Science should be raised in this great centre of thought and education. She then switched over to two faculties of brain—the analytical and the one which synthesises and she hinted at the presence of the third faculty. In this way, she, as if, built an edifice step by step deeply rooted in the Vedic thought and *mantras*. She started with the basic idea of the cosmos, cosmology and cosmogony as enshrined in the Vedas. I was reminded of the *mantras* which we recite everyday in our *sandhyopāsanā* and on various other occasions.

These *mantras* are deeply linked with the notion of Ṛta, i.e. the cosmic order, the ritualistic or sacrificial order wherefrom the entire ethical moral order arises and from Ṛta emerges the cosmic water which again manifests itself into the time. Then it has been described how from temporarily, the entire universe of the form and the space emerges. Thereafter she dealt, step by step, with the emergence of entire universe of the *pañcamahābhūtas*. Then she powerfully relates it to rational understanding of the entire thought implicitly present in the Vedic idea of Cosmic order.

Through reason, we can intellectually understand the Vedic view of Universe, for there is no dichotomy in entire thought tradition between the Pratibhā and Tarka. There is the possibility of analysis and yet another possibility of synthesis of the two as she argues that they are not two opposites. She did it by referring to Mahāmahopādhyāya Lakshmana Shastri Joshi. She pointed out that in the Vedic myths this idea is reflected in the concept of *mithuna*. She emphasized that there is not the idea of the conflict, i.e. the *dwandwa* which forms the essence of the Vedic myth. The area of the myth is formed by the idea of *mithuna* where two are not only related, rather two are indivisible. Therefore, the third notion in the Vedic thought. She has pointed out, how does it percolate in entire Indian culture. She has demonstrated how right from the *apas* to the *nāgas*, from the *mahābhutas* to the living beings, the unity is laid down. I do not think I have any more to speak on this count. Now this is not the area which should be touched.

With her permission, I would like to switch over to another side. How the confusion arises in Indian mind. What is the background of the confusion about the nature of Vedic Myths and the Mythology created in the people educated under modern system.

By the end of eighteenth century when the British Imperialism has been fully established in India, a noted scholar, namely Sir William Jones joins Calcutta High Court and devotes his time in cultivating his own Sanskrit language. As a result, it strikes to him that there is some fundamental relationship between the Sanskrit and the family of languages starting from Greek, Latin, old German to old Iranian. He chose a few cognate words from all these languages and writes his paper which not only generates a keen interest in the European mind for Sanskrit, but also opens a gate for the emergence of a new discipline called 'Comparative and Historical Philology.' With this new discipline, a new methodology of interpreting the Sanskrit text is evolved and study of the Vedas takes place in the West. By the middle of the nineteenth century, some of the German scholars claimed that this new methodology based on comparative and historical philology was sufficient for the interpretation of Vedic texts so much so that they need not apply traditional Indian method for the interpretation of the Vedic texts. Scores of Western scholars tried to interpret the Vedas and the mythology enshrined in these texts. Mostly their interpretation ignored the traditional Indian methodology based on the works of Yāska, Śaunaka, the Vedāṅgas as well as the later commentaries on Vedas. The text originating from a different tradition and the application of the methodology developed in an alien tradition resulted into a very wide gap between the text and its interpretation. The same happened with the interpretation of the myths and legends enshrined in the Vedas as well as the later texts including Purāṇas. People educated under the modern system have been generally familiar with the Western interpretation only. Therefore, the widening of the gap between the Indian mythology and its interpretation continues. Happily, there are few exceptions among the Western scholars who have successfully rectified the mistake and they have offered their interpretation quite in tune with the Indian understanding of the myths. Heinrich Zimmer, Stella Kramrisch and others may be mentioned among the Western scholars and Anand Coomaraswamy, Yogiraj Aurobindo, Vasudev Sharan Agrawal, Vidya Niwas Mishra and Kapila Vatsyayan may be cited among the Indian scholars.

The deeper interest in the Vedas of the Western scholars resulted further in the emergence of the discipline called 'Comparative Mythology.' In the later half of the nineteenth century, there was the emergence of the anthropology and it concentrated its attention on mythologies of the world The mythologies were seen as the creation of the primitive mind. During this period, the scholars like Usener, Bloomfield, Max Müller, Macdonell showed a keen interest in interpreting the Vedic mythology as well as Vedic religion. Usener held the view that Vedic gods are basically the 'Departmental gods' representing the various insentient aspects as well as forces of nature. Vedic mythology is deeply rooted in this notion of religiosity. Later, Bloomfield and Macdonell developed this idea further. Bloomfield divided the Vedic gods in three categories: (1) the transparent gods, (2) the translucent gods, and (3) the opaque gods. By transparent gods, he means the gods in whose nature their basis in the nature is transparently seen such as *vāyu* (wind), *agni* (fire), *apas* (water) and *parjanya* (clouds) and so on. The translucent gods are those where their basis in nature is dimly present. For instance, Indra. The opaque gods are those where this basis is completely unrecognizable. Such as Prajāpati and others. Macdonell more or less followed Bloomfield. Such a view of Vedic gods and the idea of Vedic religion to simply worship the insentient departments and the forces of nature resulted into a very gross understanding of the Vedic myths and mythology. Apparently, this notion is based on the erroneous understanding of Vedic view of the Universe. Vedic view of the Universe is an integral and holistic one. Therefore, the presence of aspects of nature may not be ruled out whenever it is necessary, but it cannot be taken simply confined to worship of the gross and insentient aspects as well as forces of nature only. An integral and holistic view of Universe presupposes the unity of the Universe, the presense of the *cetanā,* Supreme principle behind the aspects and forces of nature. The question of the nature of Vedic gods has been raised by Yāska, Śaunaka as well as Bādarāyaṇa Vyāsa, the author of the *Brahmasūtra*. The Vedic gods are the deities presiding over the aspects and the forces of nature. It is true but the apparent multiplicity of gods is submerged into one non-dualistic 'Sat' who manifests himself as many and therefore Śaṅkarācārya interprets rightly the *Bādarāyaṇa Sūtra* 'अभिमानिव्यपदेषात्तु सिद्धम्' and he maintains that these gods are *cetanavatī devatā*. They are not simply insentient aspects and forces of the nature.

Once we realise this fundamental position of the Vedic religion and Vedic mythology, our understanding of the Vedic myths becomes different from that of most of the Western scholars. We are able to recognize the physical basis of the myths wherever they are present but at the same time these myths are much more subtle and complex. Hence we must be very careful while interpreting these myths and symbols in Vedas, Itihāsas and Purāṇas. In fact, their deeply symbolic nature has been emphasized by the scholars like Madhusudan Ojha, Vasudev Sharan Agrawal and Yogiraj Aurobindo. Madhusudan Ojha has tried to understand the Vedic mythology also in terms of modern sciences. The meaning of these mythologies are coached in a very mystic language which Madhusudan Ojha and Vasudev Sharan Agrawal interpret on the basis of the Āraṇyakas. Yogiraj Aurobindo opts for unfolding the deeper meanings of the Vedic myths and symbols relating them to deeper spiritual meanings. Anand Coomaraswamy opens a way to go even deeper into meanings of the Vedic mythology.

The myths enshrined in the Veda have been expanded and interpreted in the Itihāsas like the *Rāmāyaṇa* and the *Mahābhārata* and Purāṇas. The speculations on the Vedic mythology find elaborate treatment in the Brāhmaṇa texts and the interpretations of the Vedic myths appearing in the Itihāsas and Purāṇas owe much to the Āraṇyakas and Brāhmaṇas. Therefore, it is the *upabṛnhaṇa* (expansion) of the Veda.

The myths are known in our language as *khyāna,* i.e. the narratives. Their narrative character has also to be kept in our mind when we are trying to collect the scientific data from the myths which are deeply rooted in the cosmogony and cosmology from which they spring forth. However, it cannot be denied that some valuable facts may be derived from the careful study of Indian myths and symbols and Vedic and Pauranic mythology which may expand our understanding in terms of modern sciences, especially the question of the origin of Cosmos. However, it may be done with some caution so that we may reach the Universal truth without compromising with the real meanings of the myths.

2

Ecology and Indian Myth[1]

Kapila Vatsyayan

In October 1977 an Inter-governmental Conference on Environmental Education was held in Tbilisi, Georgia, USSR. The declaration began with the following words:

> In the last few decades man has, through his power to transform his environment, wrought accelerated changes in the balance of nature. The result is frequent exposure of living species to dangers which may prove irreversible.[2]

It was a significant coincidence that the Conference should have been held in Georgia, USSR, because by some accounts, major Indo-Aryan migrations of man took place from this region to the sub-continent of India. It was man+men from these regions who settled in India ultimately gave India the most complete holistic perspective of the Universe. The cosmology, the science and philosophy, in short the total worldview, has been sustained by this civilisation through millennia. The Man-Nature relationship was at the core of this vision enunciated repeatedly at all dimensions—biological, physical, psychical, philosophical, metaphysical and spiritual. All life was interrelated and inter-woven: the process of transmutation and cyclic degeneration and regeneration of life was a perennial postulate.

We have come a long, long way since then. Despite the traditional holistic view embedded in each and every discipline, articulated through sacred incantations and systemised as ritual for constant reminder of the need to sustain and foster the ecological balances of nature, we stand at the threshold of disaster in a manner never before faced by Man, who as the Tbilisi declaration states, has 'used his power to transform his environment'. We may even substitute the word 'transform', with words like 'conquer', 'destroy', 'desecrate', 'plunder', so as to bring home the fact that a single factor of Man who can be distinguished from all living matter through his distinctive power to reflect, to articulate and be wise, has been the very instrument of these ecological imbalances—imbalances which threaten the very existence of Man. As one eminent scientist-philosopher put it in the context of India: "Even more than population explosion, the imbalances in the environment and ecology are the greatest threat to the continent. We may be able to control the first, but the process of devastation we have begun in the second may bring final doom".

The question to be asked is, what are the diverse components of the disturbance, the ecological imbalances and what methodologies and strategies were adopted in the past to sustain these balances. Can we, even at this stage, learn any lessons from the past for equipping ourselves to face the human predicaments today?

Let us begin by enumerating the principal components of the environment most polluted, species most threatened and how each disturbs the ecological balance. Thereafter, we can return to the worldview of the historical past, the myth, ritual and art of this country or for that matter, practically all cultures, pre-renaissance. The worldview is mercifully sustained by so-called primitive societies, be it in India, Africa, Australia or America. At the philosophic, speculative level, the living continuities can be seen only in India.

So today, this moment where four-fifth of humanity lives (i.e. India and Asia), what is threatened? What are we polluting, destroying, thus bringing forebodings of the annihilation of Man on earth? What is the quality of life we can hope for?

First and foremost is water, the basic sustaining principle—clean water or to use a traditional phrase 'pure or unpolluted (*shuddha*) water'—which is becoming scarce. Water systems are increasingly overexploited and polluted. Any Indian is familiar with the daily rituals which serve as reminders of the concept of pure and, therefore, holy water. No daily, monthly, annual ceremony is complete without ritual purification with water. At birth, marriage, death, this concept is articulated and yet we have polluted these waters of life.

The next, pollution of the earth—Mother Earth, floating free ball beneath the most gleaming membrane of bright blue sky. And what have we done to it? Arid lands have increased, soil which was venerated has been eroded and infertility, sand and salt have taken over. It is estimated that in this part of the world, a million hectares are being desertified each year. Desecration of the bowels of the earth through excessive quarrying is common. Man's power has asserted its most destructive tendencies and the collective greed of Man has hollowed the still centre of life. *Prithvi,* the eternal mother, has been polluted and desecrated.

Related to the pollution of water and earth is the massive unprecedented deforestation. The Indian sub-continent has been progressively deforested, the soil's ability to absorb and hold water has diminished. Severe floods have occurred more frequently and deforestation has affected most adversely the eco-system of the Himalayas where our major river systems—the Indus, the Ganges and the Brahmaputra—originate. Each day we learn of the increase in wastelands and their consequent effect upon rural life, be they the forests of Bastar or the hills of the Himalayan range. In the language of Indian myth, this is the rape of the tree and river goddess, the *Vrikshikas*, and the destruction of the gods of the woods, the *Vanadevata*. No wonder the Chipko Movement and the Project Silent Valley is a cry of anguish. Most of all, the present destruction is dangerous play with the mythical centre—*Sumeru*, the world axis, the Himalayas.

The disturbance in water, earth, vegetation, river and mountain ecology systems, has naturally threatened all manners of life—aquatic, terrestrial and celestial. Mythically, *Seshanaga* upholds the earth, the Ganga rides the crocodile, Jamuna the tortoise and each is threatened. Boars and elephants upheld the earth; they too are dying. So who upholds the earth now? The birds of heaven, the Swan, the Garuda and others, which carried the gods are vanishing. So who sustains the moral and cosmic order? There can only be chaos.

And worst of all, there is the pollution of the holy space—the air (*Vayu*), and the sky—which permeates and envelopes all life. The tragedy of Bhopal is too close for comment, but equally demonic are the asuric chimneys of black tamasic forces which pollute the 'lung' of life. Acid rain are common elsewhere and man looks in vain for the purity of the water to flow from the rain-filled clouds. Destruction is writ large on the balmy skies, once azure blue, today smoke grey.

Finally, we have polluted holy sound, the primeval *nada*, through the chaos of our life. Noise pollution makes Man deaf to the inner voices of his wisdom.

And so Man aspires higher and higher, beyond the pollution of his making, to that one source which sustains all and is yet beyond his reach, namely the Sun—*Aditya*—the giver of light in the sky and fire on earth—*Agni*—the source of energy which appears unpollutable unlike the fuel of his making. This energy, physically and metaphysically, is Man's only ray of hope for the continuance of life.

The brief description given above can be multiplied a hundredfold to underline the disastrous effects of wind and land erosion, the infertility of soil, disturbance of bio-ecology of aquatic, terrestrial and celestial life, and to speak of the pollution of the *Sushumna nadi*, the central artery of the Indo-Gangetic plains—the Ganga.

But perhaps these illustrative examples will suffice to convince us that stated differently or stated in the traditional language understood by the literate and illiterate of this country, Man has disturbed the cosmic order, the rhythm of the movement of the earth, water, fire, ether and *Agni* (*Surya*), i.e. the five elements, where inter-action, inter-connection and inter-weaving was the rule rather than the exception. The sustenance of the ecological balance was Man's first and last duty, for only then the moral order of the world *Ṛta* as also *Dharma* in their fundamental connotation could be or would be sustained. The emphasis was both on the notion of purity and non-pollution as also on ecological balance. Any assertion of greed or power disturbed the balance, and this is the story of all those who are called *Asuras* in mythical terms. Restraint in the use of power was the central message.

My limited purpose here is to revive the collective physical memory of this heritage, to draw attention to the myths, art and ritual, science, religion and philosophy in India, that were the strategies through which this holistic worldview of ecological balance was articulated.

Cutting across historical developments, philosophic debates, scientific controversies, religious sects and cults, the one principle which underlies and provides unity as also continuity of vision and perception is the assertion that Man is only one among all living matter, in short, the notion of the *Jiva*. Man's life depends upon and is conditioned by all that surrounds him and sustains him, namely inanimate, mineral and animate, aquatic, vegetative, animal and gaseous life. It is, therefore, Man's duty to constantly remind himself—in individual and collective life—of the environment and the ecology. Such veneration is no animistic primitive fear; it is wisdom contained in the language of myth and symbol. Their efficacy lies in their capacity of multiple interpretations at the biological function, societal, philosophic and religious levels. The pivot around which Indian myth moves, not unlike that of other parts of ancient world, is ecological balance.

Developments in Indian science, specially mathematics, chemistry, biology, owe their systems to this holistic worldview of ecological balance. The philosophic systems, whether from the polarity of the realist Charaka or the Sankhya, assert it, the language of Indian myth and art manifests it in an unparalleled lucidity of narrative statement and depth of thought, meaning and a clarity of message which has a validity here and now.

Although we can discuss separately the five principal components of the environment or what in traditional language are called the five basic elements of water, earth, air, space and fire, which comprise the microcosm of the biological Man as also the macrocosm of the universe, it must be remembered that no single element is autonomous. It is in their ecological interaction that they assume significance.

Let us begin with primary elements. First, the water that sustains life, the first principle of fertility and of life whether of ocean or river or clouds or sky. The archaeological evidences of Mohenjodaro, Harappa, Lothal and the recent excavations of Ganga Valley leave no doubt about the fundamental ritual importance accorded to water and its fecundity. The Vedas devote many hymns to waters. Mythically, Varuna is the god of the waters; he is considered the great superintendent of the cosmic moral order (*Ṛta*); he is the guardian of the West. In a hymn dedicated to Varuna in the *Atharvaveda* (IV. 16), it is said:

> This earth is King Varuna's as also this great-flung sky, the two seas are his belly (appetite); at the same time he is hidden in this little water. Even we who may cross the sky will not escape King Varuna; from heaven his spies are patrolling this earth with a thousand eyes; they scan through the earth. King Varuna sees all that is between heaven and earth and that which is beyond (them).

Perhaps there is no need to decode the myth. In saying that Varuna's sphere is the earth and heaven and in the waters, the Vedic poet is referring to an eternally known natural phenomenon of the primeval waters rising as vapour (as spies) in the sky only to descend again to Earth. Understandably, the emblem of Varuna is 'fish', his vehicle the crocodile, the wind is his breath (as *Dikpala Vayu* wind is the guardian of the North-West). He spans boundless paths for the sun and ensures that the rivers fall into the ocean. He knows the paths of ships on the ocean and the flight of birds in the sky. He punishes those who transgress his laws.

Indeed, in the Indian worldview, as also of other ancient civilisations and cultures, life on earth emerges from the eternal waters that hold the potency of fire: the two together transform into forms of world, mineral, plant, animal and divine. From the primeval waters emerge stones in the shapes of ovoid pebbles and spheres with ammonites going back to millions of years. Many a devout Indian is familiar with *banalingas* and *shalagramas* which are sought and collected for worship. Perhaps the modern Indian has not paused to ponder over the significance of the myth of the Varuna, the vigilant superintendent, and the symbolic ecological significance of the *banalingam* and *shalagramas*. Stated differently, they articulate an intuitive scientific comprehension or wisdom through a conceptual parallel in imaginative form. While on the surface, myth has a dream-like structure, its meaning and value lie in its pointing at natural phenomenon. As has been pointed out, Indian science and philosophy and thus its symbols developed on the postulate of the perpetual movement of creation, degeneration and regeneration of the cosmos. This is quite distinct from an evolutionary model. Time and existence are conceived of as systems of inter-connected cycles, not in linear terms starting from one specific divine act of creation. Resultantly, Indian cosmology tends to be circular or what was the fluid within is the ocean.

It is obvious that intuitively, without perhaps empirical verification and analysis, this is an ecological statement through metaphor of the greatest significance. The *banalinga* from the Narmada, i.e. waters, and the *shalagramas*, i.e. the ammonite fossils coming from the mountains, are the concrete symbols of the creation from the waters and solar energy. The radial lines and a projecting centre of the the *shalagramas* point at the latter. Equally widespread is the myth of their personifying the horizontally floating golden egg, i.e. Vishnu himself lying upon an undulating serpent which represents the inexhaustible primordial ocean of *pralaya.* The symbolic significance of these simple stones reflects a sensitive comprehension of ecology, specially when it is further said that fire rises from the waters or the sun from the ocean. In sum, the waters and these stones are a meditative help, leading to a comprehension of continuous evolution and devolution process of all time and existence.

The myths of waters take innumerable other forms relating to the ocean (*sagar*), the rivers and the nymphs of the skies. Indian literature is replete with their names—Saraswati, Ganga, Yamuna, Urvashi or Menaka. Indian folklore sanctifies these. All these deities are members of the vast water cosmogony so vital and central to Indian thought. Little wonder that from the simplest tribal to the most sophisticated Indian venerates water in some form or the other. Rituals of purity of waters are known to all parts of India. The Indian is familiar with the common (but little understood today) custom of a full pitcher greeting guests and being kept at the entrance of the house. Has he reflected over what cosmic significance this may hold?

From Varuna, let us turn our attention to the great river systems of India, i.e. Indus, Ganga and Brahmaputra. Countless myths have been woven around the eco-system of these rivers—sensitive, meaningful stories narrate imaginatively the ecological movements. As an example, from the vast storehouse of these myths, we chose the most familiar one which has sustained Indian life and one most polluted. Our anxiety for its physical purity is obvious in the establishment of the Ganga Authority. But let us see how she dominates Indian myth and cosmogony from earliest times. Jawaharlal Nehru had called her a symbol of India's age-long culture and civilisation, ever-changing, ever-flowing, and yet ever the same Ganga. The late Indira Gandhi did not consider it strange that the "Ganga should have such an extraordinary hold on the imagination of the peoples of India. For millennia, she has watered and nurtured an entire civilisation, and has become a symbol of eternity—a theme of art, myth, legend and literature. The moods of rivers are fascinating to watch but even more so are the faith and reverence they evoke in the heart of millions".

And what is the myth of creation of this great river the Ganga and how has she captured the imagination?

Ganga like the *shalagramas* and the floating egg on the serpent of undifferentiated waters continue to be related to serpents, crocodiles, and aquatic life. In Indian myth and iconography, she often assumes a mermaid form protected by a hood of snakes.

If Varuna has spies in heaven, Ganga descends from heaven. She is the holy water in the *kamandala* of Brahma which purifies the world; she descends from the heavens from the foot of Vishnu as *Trivikrama* when he traversed the three orders of space, nether, terrestrial and celestial, with his three steps, but most important she is the drop of water from the celestial heaven which fills the ocean (*sagar*). The descent of the Ganga from the heavens evolves through centuries in the form of an elaborate, ecologically charged myth.

Several versions of the myth are found in the *Ramayana*, *Mahabharata* and the several Puranas, while details of names of saints and heroes differ in many cases and sometimes become localised. Central to the myth is the connection of the ocean and the sky and the channelisation of river systems through human effort. In traditional language, it is the story of the King of Oceans (*sagara*); the Milky Way of the sky, Ganga; the saint Agastya; the *tapas* or austerities of Bhagiratha, the Man; and the forests of the locks of Shiva.

In one version, Agastya, who, in some ways, is related to solar energy, once swallowed the entire ocean. Although he meant well as he wanted to expose the demons hiding in the sea, it had the effect of depriving the earth and all beings of the necessary life-sustaining water. This made it necessary for the celestial river, a kind of Milky Way, to descend from the sky.

Now it fell to the share of another human, a pious Bhagiratha to undertake great austerities so as to bring the heavenly Ganga to earth. He was sorely in need of water to appease and gratify the ashes and souls of his deceased forefathers who had perished in a similar natural catastrophe of drought. Leaving the administration of his kingdom to his ministers, he left for a place in south India called Gokarna (cow's ear). With unflinching determination and perseverance, he practised austerities, *tapas*, through discipline and commitment. Eventually, Brahma was pleased and promised to grant him a wish. Bhagiratha asked the god to let Ganga descend to earth. Brahma agreed but drew attention to the necessity of soliciting Shiva's help and grace. He feared that if the mighty river of heaven with her torrential waters were to descend directly, it may cleave the earth and shatter it. Someone would have to break the fall by receiving the gigantic cataract on his head. This only Shiva could do. Bhagiratha once again continued his austerities until the god was appeased. He stood on one leg with his arms uplifted (*urdhvabahu*); he practised the penance of the five fires (*panchatapas*) and finally Shiva appeared and acquiesced. The head of the great god took the first full impact of Ganga's torrential flow. The matted hair of the *jatas* piled high, delayed the cascading current which then in meandering through the labyrinths of the forest of his *jatas* lost its force, was tamed and channelised. Its water descended gently to the Himalayas and then, majestically, to the Indian plains, and thus the earth and its creatures were rejuvenated, for she was the life-giving boon.

The ecological messages of the myth are as clear as the physical reality of the course of the Ganga; its origin in the Himalayas, whether mythically Kailash or actually Gomukha or Gangotri, the Vasudhara falls and the rich Deodar forests through which it meanders, the several streams into which it breaks before reaching Haridwar (literally the entrance of Hara Shiva). What is sanctified in the myth is both the ecological process as also the power of austere discipline to uphold the moral and ecological order and not to destroy it. Man, if he so wills, can accumulate an immense reservoir of physical and psychical energy through concentration and discipline. *Tapas* is the power, armour or commitment that becomes a high power electric charge, which in a flash can cut through and melt all resistance. Today, Man's *tapas* lies in keeping the great river pure and clean at the source and through all its meandering journey through the forests, plains, fields, villages and cities, till it is again received by the ocean (*sagar*). The celestial skies are the pilgrim centres of Kailash, Gomukha or Gangotri which must be nurtured, the locks of Shiva are the Himalayan forests which must tame the river so as to avoid wrathful floods and landslides, and the *tapas* of Man is the exercise of his selective discriminating power for using water for hydro-electric energy. The ecological connection of the North and the South and their inter-connected systems is reflected by Bhagiratha's undertaking his austerities in Gokarna in the South.

The myth is elaborated in many ways in all regions of India and throughout Indian history. It assumes paramount significance on account of the present state of pollution. The work of scientists, programmes of afforestation, rural and urban sewage systems have only to reach out for support and reinforcement in Indian art. Indeed, Indian architecture,

Fig. 2.1. *Ganga-avataran* Panel. Mamallapuram. (Courtesy: Archaeological Survey of India)

sculpture and painting is the most effective, aesthetically pleasing, symbolically loaded message totally contemporary and valid statement of the ecology and concern—if only it could be utilised. To use an inelegant phrase, the great temples of India, ranging from Badrinath, to Gangaikonda-Cholapuram, to the countless figures of Ganga riding a crocodile, surrounded by aquatic life-sustaining creatures are the natural hoardings of mass media only if we had eyes to see and a mind to comprehend, and ears to hear the incantation of thousands to Ganga as *sukhada* and *mokshada*. Countless images and *mantras* lie all over India in every nook and corner from Assam to Rajasthan and Gujarat, Kashmir to Kanyakumari. Are they hollow and ineffective? Can new meaning and significance not be given?

Surpassing in stature, beauty and ecological significance is the monumental dramatic relief of all time in Mamallapuram. It represents the celebrated myth of the descent of the Ganga in a manner which leaves an indelible impression. On a huge wall of rock rising vertically towards the clear blue skies of south India, a cosmic tableaux in relief is enacted on a space of twenty-seven metres length, nine in height (Fig. 2.1). It is teaming with hosts of serpents, plants, animals, men, women, *apsaras* and *gandharvas*, all converging towards a natural cleft in the middle of the composition. The decisive moment of the effectiveness of Bhagiratha's *tapas* no doubt dramatically captured, but what is more, the series of events or ecological phases are all depicted in one setting. The celestial stream rushed down metaphorically through a cistern above the great rock. Today we imagine this stream. A giant serpent king (*nagaraja*) is covered by the torrent, moves upward in undulating movements, i.e. all aquatic life rejoices at her descent. To the right of the saint are large aquatic birds, large geese. All manners of life flock together—reptiles, animals, birds, gods and goddesses. Here are elephants, families of perching monkeys, deers, lions, *apsaras* and *gandharvas*—all watch the miracle. In a superb animated sculptural style, this is the true celebration and consecration of life, asserting, reaffirming the basic kinship of all living creatures. All is sustained by one life source, one life-giving energy; this is universal-eternal play of matter and energy. The waters of the dried *sagara* descend from heaven to purify all.

One could go on ad infinitum not only about the myth and this serpent relief, but about the innumerable masterly examples of Ganga and of Shiva, as Gangadhara and Ganga, as woman descending through the dance movement called *Ganga-avataran*.

But from the Ganga water, we must move to the first vegetative and aquatic life principle. The lotus and the snake in botanical and zoological terms are born of the waters. In mythical terms, the lotus emerges from the primeval waters, whether river or pond. It is the most important of vegetative forms born of water, connected to the mythical centre of the earth through its stem, and always above the water; its leaf the symbol of untainted purity, its flower blossoming with fragrance. Physically, the lotus is a typical ecological statement of the processes of nature. Symbolically, it assumes the greatest importance in Indian myth, art and ritual. The metaphor of the lotus leaf, the lotus flower and stem permeates Indian literature in practically all languages. If the motif of the lotus was excluded from Indian *mantra, tantra, yantra,* poetry, prose, music, dance, sculpture, monumental as the free-standing pillars with inverted lotus or relief as the magnificent panels in Sanchi or Indian painting, the Indian heritage would be impoverished beyond recognition.

The lotus is a comparatively late entrant into Indian myth, but once it finds a place, Hindu, Jain, Buddhist art, thought and myth, consider it indispensable. In all cases, whether as seat (*asana)* or as emblem or epithet, it denotes fecundity, abundance, well-being. Logically, lotus becomes goddess and is personified as *Sri* and *Lakshmi*. She is praised as lotus-born (*padmasambhava*), standing on a lotus (*padmasthita*), lotus coloured (*padmavarna*), lotus-thighed (*padmauru*), lotus-eyed (*padmaksi*), abounding in lotuses (*padmini*), decked with lotus garland (*padmamalini*), and a thousand other names. We are familiar with *Bodhisattva Padmapani*, the female as *prajna* counterpart, *parmita* who sits on a lotus and holds a lotus. Underlying this preoccupation with lotus as symbol, is the sheer physical reality of the lotus, ultimately the lotus and its petals are the multiplicity of form. Its centre corresponds to the centre of the universe, the navel of the earth, all is held together by the stem and the eternal waters. Tantric physiology regards the nervous system as a series of lotuses, and the sacred geometry of lotus is called the *Sriyantra*.

The life of the waters is intrinsically related to that of other species, the first creations of nature, namely the reptiles. Just as the lotus connects earth, water and air, so also the reptiles represent that moment of transition. All ancient religions have given a special significance to the snake. The coiled and intertwined snake represents a moment in the undifferentiated condition of creation on which human life rests. The snake is the symbol of this interconnection—swift, silent, limbless and deadly. The sign of transition is vital to man, who must be assured that this world is a cohesive unity, he cannot exist either in chaos or isolation. Thus, Vishnu at the moment before the creation of the universe, is depicted lying in a yogic sleep upon the serpent *Ananta* (Endless) with its multiple cobra heads forming a canopy. Man and reptile as man and water and vegetation are inter-related and inter-dependent.

The countless myths relating to snakes again pervade the Indian psyche in all regions, all levels of society giving rise to major cults which have great ecological significance. Its detailed unfolding could fill volumes. In art, *Nagas* and *Naginis* abound in Hindu, Buddhist and Jain art. In a beautiful relief of the Shunga period (Pauni, Maharashtra), beneath the Boddhi tree, the multi-headed cobra, King Muchilinda, rises up to protect the seated Buddha. Eastern India deifies the snake goddess as Manasa. Badami caves have the coiled serpent as the eternal movement of cyclic time on the ceiling and the coiled *Naga* from the Chalukyan period is a perfect geometric statement of the lotus *Naga*, water and earth.

The snakes and reptiles in a dramatic moment of biological mutation acquire wings and become birds. They are inter-related antagonist and

Fig. 2.2. Ganga mounting *Makara*. Ellora. (Courtesy: Archaeological Survey of India)

yet complementary. Intuitively, the Indian sees this ecological connection and Indian myth provides many examples of reptiles changing to birds or reptiles and birds seemingly antagonistic to each other being vehicles of gods. Thus, Vishnu lies on the *Ananta Sheshanaga* and he rides the Garuda. The animals follow suit, and the entire range of evolution, from the hare to the lion, from the rodent to the primate, is vividly represented. They crowd the outer walls and lower lintels of Indian stupas and temples by the hundred, sometimes in processional rows, in pairs, or yet again in conjunction with trees, floral motifs, and as conjoined images of fantasy. Occasionally they are aquatic, as in the mythical crocodile (*makara)* who is the vehicle of Ganga (Fig. 2.2); at other times, they are of the earth or the desert, as are the elephants and lions; while others are monkeys who befriend man.

Amongst the creations of fantasy are the mythical lion or tiger, the *shardula;* more fearsome is the *vyala,* the vicious beast. These mythic animals appear either in isolation or in conjunction with dwarfs and women on temple walls, guarding sanctuaries. These are also the many-winged animals called *suparnas*. Each animal acquires its own symbolism, and by the fourth century they develop into a systematised pantheon closely related to the world of humans and celestials. Most Indian sculptures are structured to comprehend the world of aquatic, plant, animal and human life. Each is an aspect of the other; superficially they appear as decoration, yet at a deeper level, the aquatic, vegetative, and animal elements represent aspects of the human psyche. Metamorphosis and transmutation are logical and traditional. This rich abundance of nature, its manifold creations and organic coherence, logically culminate in the universal fertility theme known to all ancient religions.

But we must pass on to the next most important element of environment which has provided the world with vast oceans of myth. Earth is known to all civilisations and cultures as the great Mother Goddess. Predating the Vedas are the figures of Mother Earth Goddess in the form of ring stones. The Vedas dedicate many hymns to *Prithvi*, the *Prithvisūtra* being one of the greatest hymns. She is invoked as born of the waters of the ocean. Surrounded by space, she is the creator, the sustainer. In the *Atharvaveda* there is a prayer which draws attention once again to ecological balances and how the earth, like Varuna, is the upholder of the moral order. Like the river goddess, she repesents fecundity. Truth and moral order sustain her. She is the mistress of past and future, giver of the wide and wildlife world of human life. She has high heights, stretches on level ground, reaches to the sea, bears herbs of manifold potency, on whom food and crops grow and animals roam whom Indra from the sky fertilises, that earth is invoked as Mother. Man says:

> I am the son of the earth, the rains are my father, let him, the Lord of the rain, fill the Earth for us. O Earth, protect us, purify us. Let people milk her with amity. O Earth, give us sweet words. The snowy mountain heights and thy forests, O Earth, shall be kind to us and we to them.

What could be more lucid ecological statement of the intrinsic relationship of water, earth, air, sky and sun, and Man? As in the case of water, the emphasis is on purification-purity, i.e. non-pollution.

Her fertility is symbolised through the image of the brimming vase, the bowl of plenty. Foliage and the lotus emerge from the bowl: the waters below the life-giving forces of regeneration and energy of sun blossom as the vegetation is the sap of life (the *rasa*). Water, earth, plant, animal, human and the divine come together in images of the Goddess *Prithvi*, also identified as *Devi.*

Prithvi, the Mother Earth, sustains plant life in all its multitudinous variety. Volumes could be written on the veneration of plants, forests and herbs in India. The tree is sacred to one and all. In the Himalayas, the *Deodar* is considered the abode of the gods; one may cut a tree only at his own peril; when they were felled, it was with due ceremony. Plural planting was the norm. The *Sal* is equally venerated in Uttar Pradesh, Bihar and Madhya Pradesh. The forests of *Deodar* and *Sal*, the flowering *Asoka*, the *Bilva*, the *Kadamba*, the *Rudraksha*, the *Parijata*, the *Champak* are all sacred. So also are *Palasha*, *Amaltas* and *Ketki*. The *Ashwatha*, *Banyan*, *Neem*, coconut palm and bamboo are ecologically important and mythically central; herbs of all varieties, the *Tulsi*, the *Kesar* and grass, *Durvagha*s to *Munja* are venerated.

Have we paused to question why the Indian psyche paid this attention to trees, herbs, plants and related them to characters, namely divine, human, seasons, moods, *rasas*, *bhavas*? It is these life-giving plants and trees where the gods dwell who have been vital and crucial for maintenance of ecological balances who we have desecrated and destroyed. Myths evolved around each and every one of these trees and

Fig. 2.3. *Varaha* Panel. Udayagiri (Courtesy: Vidula Jayaswal)

plants. *Ashwatha* was central, so also was *Bilva,* the mango, the *Sal,* the coconut and the bamboo. If one was the tree of life, the other was of the upturned tree of Upanisadic thought. The *Sal* is not only central and vital to the ecological cycle of the forests of Bihar and Bastar providing vast communities with the famous Karma festival, but it is the *Sal* tree which *Maya* embraced as the Buddha was born. The significance of the coconut tree is botanical, functional, nutritional and mythical in ritual terms and it is too well known to need recounting.

In Udayagiri, the myth of Prithvi is carved in stone (Fig. 2.3). This time the Varaha, the bear in mundane terms, the wild pig, the scavenger of the terrestrial space, rescues her from the deluge. Vishnu Varaha rises from the waters where cosmic upheavals have taken place. In the relief the gigantic Varaha rises from the waters, seen as incised wavy patterns, unruffled and effortlessly lifts Prithvi Mother Goddess with garland and lotus stalk (Fig. 2.3). His monumental body, the strong legs, the posture of *alidha* are in contrast with the delicacy and kindness with which he lifts Prithvi. A total cosmic drama is enacted in monumental proportions in stone as in Mamallapuram where the *joviga* myth is recreated in plastic form of all proportions.

The Udayagiri relief is another powerful statement of ecological balance where the waters, the *Nagas*, the animals and human are inter-connected. The Varaha deity represents the primeval organic relationship of animal and humans—so necessary for conserving the life energy of our planet.

The tree-woman relationship dominates Indian Myth. The most functionally meaningful and inspirer of countless myths and the richest treasure of Indian sculptural motif is the *Vrishkika*, also called by other names—*Yakshi, Surasundari* and many others. They stand against trees, embrace them and thus become an aspect of the tree articulating the interpretation of the plant and the human. The tree is dependent upon the woman for its fertility as is the woman on the tree.

These *Vrishkikas* or *Yakshis* are the creatures of the water, earth, plant and human. No wonder in point of time the original river goddesses—principally Ganga, Yamuna and Saraswati—submerge into each other. *Yakshi* along with Ganga, Yamuna and Saraswati standing on their respective aquatic vehicles, the crocodile, tortoise and swan, are guardians of sanctuaries and prepare the devotee for the inner journey.

Furgusson considers them the pictorial representation of the primitive faiths, the casteless *Dasyus* (slaves), who inhabited northern India before the advent of the Aryans. Vögel studies them as part of *Naga* or serpent cult. Vincent Smith speaks of them as fertility goddesses, and Coomaraswamy wrote one of his earliest books on them and their male counterparts, the *Yakshas.* They are seen in Indian art from the earliest Mauryan remains (second century BC) to the medieval sculpture and painting. They are mentioned in classical Sanskrit literature, and Kalidasa centres the plot of one play *Malavikagnimitra* around the ceremony of the woman and the tree (the *Asoka dohada* motif). The myth in all its diversity of manifestation is an excellent example of a purely functional aspect of life being transmitted into myth. The *Asoka* tree is known for its medicinal

Fig. 2.4. *Salbhanjika* bracket: Sanchi (Courtesy: Vidula Jayaswal)

value in curing certain feminine diseases. Its bark and flower are used in indigenous medicine even today. The tree is essential for the natural health and regularity of women's biological system. The myth inverts the functions and transforms it into the woman's embrace being essential for the flowering of *Asoka* tree, thus the word *Asoka dohada* or the generic word *Salbhanjika* (she who leans on the tree). In some parts of India, there continues still a periodic ritual where women embrace the tree and partake of its bark or flower.

The myth then enters literature, architecture and sculpture and becomes a dominant artistic motif. Viewers of Indian art will easily recall the outstanding example of the motif in Sanchi where she performs a purely architectural function as a diagonal bracket and is the symbol of the fullness of vegetation and life (Fig. 2.4). She appears repeatedly in Indian art of all ages and regions as brackets or ceiling figures, isolated reliefs in conjunction with trees, plants and animals. The medieval temples of Khajuraho, Bhuvanesvara, the temple of Mount Abu and Ranakapura are crowded with these figures on the outer walls and as pillar or ceiling figures. While she is tree and plant, she is also the celestial beauty (the *Surasundari*) and the dancer. In plastic form she is invariably in the attitude of dance and often holds musical instruments symbolising the sound of music and harmony. She is in close proximity with animals or occasionally rides them. Nameless, she is the epitome of the inherent harmony of plant, animal and human life. She is the ecological balance between the nature and the human. The *Yakshi* is another manifestation of the goddess of the forest, the *Aranyani* of the Vedas. The poet invokes her:

> Goddess of wild and forest who
> Seemest to vanish from sight
> The goddess never slays unless
> Some murderous enemy approaches.
> Now have I praised the Forest Queen,
> Sweet scented redolent of balm
> The mother of all sylvan things,
> Who tells not but hath stores of food.

Water, earth, tree provide the basis of three distinct types of goddesses and women in myth and art. The sky, although the father, is the atmosphere which sustains other goddesses. Predominant amongst the goddesses of the atmosphere is Dawn (*Ushas)*and her companion the Night (*Ratri).* A famous hymn of the *Rigveda* invokes Dawn; she is described as a dancer who appears on the stage and unveils herself. She is the provider of light and life. The verse runs:

> Oh Ushas, nobly born
> Bestow thou on us vast and glorious riches
> Preserve us, evermore ye gods with blessings

(*RV* VI, 78,6)

and again:

> The fire well kindled
> Sings aloud to greet her
> And with their hymns
> The priests are chanting welcome
> Usha approaches in her splendour, driving
> All evil darkness far way, the goddess.

A complementary theme is that of *Ratri,* the Night. The Night too is invoked as a goddess, a *Devi,* who is the daughter of the heavens above, who pervades the worlds, who protects all beings and gives them shelter. Later this night is explained as coming forth from the *Maya* (creative power) of Brahman. She is then called *Bhuvaneswari* (the sovereign power over the worlds). The poets invoke her as follows:

> With all her eyes the goddess Night
> Looks forth approaching many a spot.
> She hath put all her glories on Immortal,
> She hath filled the waste,
> The goddess hath filled height and depth.
> She conquers darkness with her light.
> The goddess as she comes,
> Has put her sister Dawn in her place.
>
> (*RV*, X, 127, 3-8)

The Dawn and the Morning are seen in their dual divinity. The two goddesses endlessly follow similar paths but they never cross nor is there any rivalry between them. They are indeed the divine mothers of the celestial order (*Rita*).

Water, earth, tree and plant maintain the spatial balance of the cosmos, the night and dawn are the keepers of celestial temporal order and each is the goddess, mother, wife, woman or girl. They are essential for the celestial or terrestrial order, the *Rita*—a central concept of Indian cosmology and philosophic thought. At any disturbance in the order needs penance, ritual or sacrifice.

But the earth and water, the sky and the nether-world must have a centre, and hub around which the wheel moves spatially and temporally. This mythical centre is the Mount *Meru* or *Mandara* known by different names in other cosmologies.

In physical geographical terms, it is the peak of the Himalayas the Kailash and the Trishul, the ranges of Kedar and Badri. They represent the central axis. The symbol of a mountain, tree or a column situated at the centre of the world is extremely widely distributed in all ancient cosmologies, specially the Orient. Corresponding to the *Sumeru* of Indian mythology, is the concept of Haraberazait of the Iranians, Norse the Himingbjo of Mound of the Lands in the Mesopotamian tradition, Mount Tabor (Navel) and Gerizim of the Palestinian tradition and Golgotha of the Christian tradition. In India, the Kailash and the Himalayas are final journey of man's ascension; all aspire to this goal of reaching the heights and moving inward. Ecologically important, psychically and metaphorically the mountains, their height and their being equated to the centre of the cosmos naturally led to other correspondences, first the cosmic tree, then the straight column, the *yupa* of the *yajna* and ultimately the building of temples, stupas and even masjids in India, as a human endeavour, recall the experience of the Himalayas, specially the Kailash.

Kailash and Mansarovara are important pilgrimage places, consecrated and revered. Men made Kailash of Ellora, Kanchipuram and innumerable other temples concretised through rock, stone and brick the mighty all-pervasive myths of the mountain Kailash. Again in the myth, importance is attached to the mountain emerging from the egg-shaped cosmos. The slopes of this mountain are propelled by a multitude of life, creation of the water, the vegetation of the earth, forest and fields, the animals, deers, monkeys and lions, the human gnomes, dwarfs and the flying celestials. The reality and the myth are recreated in architecture for the summit of temples and stupas of Amaravati (the eternal or immortal city). Early Buddhist stupas, Bharhut, Sanchi and Amaravati are an architectural statement of the myth. Indian temples, throughout the length and breadth of India, relive the physical journey to the Kailash through the ritual circumamulation of the temple and the pilgrimage from the outer to the inner. The metaphor is logically worked out for the *shikhara* of temple rises from the hypothetical navel, the *garbhagriha,* the centre to the summit.

Whether Amarnath in Kashmir or Badrinath or Kailash, the Himalayas are the abode of the gods, particularly Shiva. He dominates the mountains as does Vishnu the waters and earth. The two, along with Brahma, are the creator, sustainer and destroyer of the universe. The mythology relating to the Himalayas is naturally intrinsically connected with the Ganga and of course the other symbol of purity, virginity, austerity—Uma, Parvati, Devi. Although Shiva appears in the Vedas only as Rudra and Satrudriya, the Puranas, specially *Siva Purana,* are full of descriptions, myths and stories full of ecological significance and meaning. In this case also, Shiva as the Lord of the Himalayas is everything and anything in the universe. He is the Lord of animals *Pasupati,* and the lord of place, *Vastospati.* Significantly, among his progeny, one belongs to the animal kingdom, Ganesa, and the other to water and fire.

Kartikeya, Somaskanda rides a peacock. Vishnu lies on the snake. Shiva rides the mighty bull, his friend and companion in effect an aspect of his nature which he must transcend. Each of these myths moves concurrently on an ecological, bio-physical and psychical plane. Each in the iconographical form is a complete ecological statement and yet none can be conceived without the other. So Shiva is incomplete in art without Shakti, Vishnu without Lakshmi, and the two are complete in the fusion of the conjoined image Hari-Hara.

The dance of Shiva is another perfect iconographical statement of ecology. What are his emblems? *Agni* and deer. What are his locks? They are the forests. Whom does he hide within himself? Ganga (water). What adorns his hair? The sun and the moon. What are his garlands? The snakes. What does he wear? The tiger skin. And what does he bring to this world? The cosmic rhythm of his *damaru* in the incessant process of cyclic creation, degeneration and regeneration and finally enlightenment of knowledge, wisdom by trampling upon the dwarf demon of darkness, ignorance and finally he blesses with the gesture of beatitude of life.

And his energy is Shakti. Without her, he is incomplete. She herself, the daughter of the Himalayas, must undergo penance and austerities. The emphasis here is like in the case of Bhagiratha on discipline and austerity, purity and concentration.

Before we finally reach that ultimate source of energy, the Sun, we have to pause to look briefly at two other elements: one *vayu* (air), and the other *akash* (space). We can only mention the other deities of the skies—the *Ashvinis* and the *Maruts*.

Many beautiful hymns are dedicated to *vayu*, the pure air. Mythically Vayu, in the Vedic pantheon, is associated with Indra; he rides the same chariot with him, indeed Indra and Vayu are often identified with each other. We know that Indra is the most powerful god of the skies and free spaces. Logically, just as Vishnu and Shiva are inter-connected and finally conjoined as Shiva-Shakti, Agni, Vayu and Śurya constitute a distinct group. The place of Agni is on earth, of *vayu* (air) or Indra in space and of Surya in heaven. Vayu is the guardian of the north-western region, and thus in close proximity to Varuna. Its indispensability is obvious: *Vayu* is limitless, effortlessly it crosses boundaries of land and sea, earth and water. Invisibly, it pervades all that lives, and without it all would die; it pervades all space, crossing the ocean and continents and is higher than the reach of fire, the flight paths of migrating birds or clouds. It is the force which protects ships across the seas or down the rivers, which moves the water and the forests, which kindles and nurtures fire, drives it forward and brings rain clouds.

Finally, air is that pure breath of life *(prana)* through the control of which man attains a state of consciousness which is at one with the *empyrean*. Like the holy waters of the Ganga, it is also the giver of *moksha*, release and emancipation. Hymns and myths of such intensity could not have been created by those who feared the elements; they were created by those who were intuitively aware of the necessity to keep the environment pure and clean within men and without. The *Vayu Purana* elaborates upon the myth here. Vayu is like Varuna and *Prithvi* is the upholder of the cosmic moral order *Rita* and *Dharma*.

Myths relating to the skies and space are innumerable. The most powerful amongst these is about Indra. He is the most important war-god. He is naturally connected with rainfall and hence thunderstorms and wields the thunderbolt. The consciousness of the life-giving function of clouds and thunder, its relation with water and fire is also common, everyday knowledge too often taken for granted without noting its significance. The companions of Indra are the twin gods Ashvin and Maruts.

And finally to that source of energy, fire, belonging to the nether, terrestrial and celestial worlds. We had already noted that the connection between water and fire in the context of the myth of Varuna. At the terrestrial level, *Agni* is venerated as the sacrificial fire of the *yajna*. The three ritual fires of the *yajna* represent the domestic, terrestrial and celestial fires. The alters are made in the shape of a semicircle, circle and square. This symbolically states the inter-connection of three order of energy. We may not try to find modern equivalents of bio-mass, bio-spheres and solar energy, but the parallels are not far to seek. Innumerable epithets suggest the many forms of *Agni*.

And finally to that great ball of fire, the Sun, to whom all aspire and which is our one ray of hope.

Like water, earth, mountain and forests, the Sun also dominates all mythologies of the ancient world.

From the pygmies of Congo to the Pharaohs of Egypt, from the Incas of Mexico and Peru, to the fire-worshippers of ancient Iran, the Sun has been a symbol of Moral light. He is again *Rita*. He takes different shapes, names and forms in different cultures and civilisations recognised as Ahura Mazda, Shamash, Helios and, of course, Apollo. In India, he is Surya, Aditya. He is the first principle of the non-manifest into the manifest. Vedic rituals consecrate through the chanting of *mantras* this light and life-giving energy. In the ritual or domestic routine of tribal and rural societies, Agni and Surya are central. Myths relating to Sun, Aditya, abound. Son of Aditi, who had eight sons, but she approached the gods with seven having cast away the eighth Martanda (the Sun). Myth and ritual on the Surya from the daily *Surya-namaskara* to the metaphysical significance of the Sun representing the process of self-awareness, has been consecrated like the Ganga, Prithvi, Himalaya in architectural edifices and sculptural statements of the deepest significance.

Temples are dedicated to the Surya in all parts of India. Martanda in Kashmir, Modhera in Gujarat, Konarak in the East. The Surya is personified as the charioteer riding the seven horses, and images of the finest quality, again made ecologically valid plastic statements of the myth, are found in all parts and in all ages.

Like the Descent of Ganga panel at Mamallapuram, the monument of supreme beauty, juxtaposed with the first principle of the mighty ocean, the open skies shrouded by vegetation and glowing with energy is Konarak, the Sun Temple. Will we maintain its purity physically, i.e. of the environs of Konarak, the cultural heritage, significance of the myth, by asking, pleading for light and life?

The energy of the Sun, the relationship of Sun, Earth, vegetation and water give rise to a whole aesthetics in India where the changing season, the *Baramasa*, the *nayakas*, the *raga* and *raginis* are all myths of ecology. Another chapter of ecology is unfolded in Indian aesthetics. We must end this article with a prayer of peace and well-being:

> Pure and peace be earth peaceful ether, peaceful heaven, peaceful
> Water, peaceful herbs, peaceful trees, may all gods
> and environs be pure and peace; may there be purity, non-pollution and
> peace through these invocations.

So the lessons are obvious. Non-pollution, discipline, restraint, awareness of inter-dependability and inter-relatedness are taught to us through custom, daily routine, myth and ritual, but we don't learn. We should learn before it is too late.

NOTES AND REFERENCES

1. The paper was published in the *India International Centre Quarterly* Issue, Vol. 19, nos. 1 and 2, 1992, on the theme 'Indigenous Vision—Peoples of India—Attitudes to the Environment', New Delhi.
2. UNESCO, UNEP Inter-Governmental Conference on Environmental Education, Tbilisi, USSR, 14-26 October, 1977, Final Report, Paris, UNESCO, 1978, p. 67.

3

Do Indian Myths Have a Scientific Basis?

P. Krishna

INTRODUCTION

According to the dictionary the word 'myth' includes several things:

(i) Completely fictional stories conjured up by a writer's imagination. These can obviously have no scientific basis.

(ii) Stories about supernatural beings usually based on religious beliefs, often referred to as 'mythology'. These are subjective and vary from culture to culture; therefore they are not universal truths and cannot have a scientific basis.

(iii) Extra-sensory perceptions: These are not anti-science and may or may not be subjective. These could be unusual records of observations and may therefore be found subsequently to have a scientific basis and be confirmed as universal truths.

THE LIMITATIONS OF SCIENCE

Science is our quest for discovering the order that manifests in Nature. We find that Nature is orderly and follows certain laws which relate causes and effects. These laws are believed to be independent of space and time. This means they are eternal and the same everywhere in the universe. It is the purpose of science to discover these laws and thereby explain the entire development of the universe. We have succeeded to a considerable extent in explaining several observed phenomena on the basis of these assumptions; therefore we believe these assumptions to be true. There has evolved a Standard Model (Weinburg, S. 1977) of the evolution of the whole universe starting from the assumption of a Big Bang which occurred some 13 billion years ago. Most scientists (though not all) accept this model to be more or less true.

There are, however, two major gaps in our understanding as it stands today:

(i) We do not know how life originated in the dead universe of the physicist starting from the Big Bang. Scientists have not been able to synthesise in the laboratory a living cell or amoeba starting from only dead chemicals or atoms. Many scientists think that life is an emergent property of matter but we do not really know. After assuming the creation of the first life form, they do have a reasonable theory of evolution to explain the origin of the myriads of living species that exist today.

(ii) We do not know what consciousness is. The scientist uses his consciousness to do his science but his science cannot explain what he is using! To pose this question in a more spectacular way, imagine that a scientist is able to synthesise my body in a chemical laboratory and put every atom in exactly the place it is at present, will he get this living person or only his dead body? Our intuition tells us that most probably he will get only the dead body. What is the difference? What is the difference between a computer and a human being? Computers have memory; they can think and calculate faster than we can in some ways. Scientists are even programming computers to respond with feelings; but a computer is not AWARE. I am aware of my body, my thoughts and my state of consciousness. Science does not know how awareness arises.

What science knows is nearly certain and has been repeatedly tested; so it is unlikely that anything that is anti-science is true. But there is a lot that is still beyond science. Consciousness phenomena like telepathy and extra-sensory perception are as yet beyond science; but we cannot say that they are unscientific or untrue.

THE SPIRITUAL QUEST

The spiritual quest of humanity is a quest for understanding the way our consciousness functions through observations and perceptions which are freed from the subjective elements of our personality. We all have within our consciousness both the personal and the universal. The personal are our thoughts and opinions, since these are based on our memory and knowledge which in turn are dependent on where we are born and grow up; but pure awareness is not so conditioned and is universal. The spiritual quest is a quest for discovering reality through awareness and direct perception freed of the subjective inputs from our personality (thought and memory).

Unfortunately, in the West, religion has come to be regarded as synonymous with belief and inquiry was suppressed as heresy. In the eastern religions there was belief, worship and ritual but there has also been a long tradition of inquiry into what is true and what is false, what is real and what is illusory. The Buddha pointed out that all sorrow (psychological suffering) is born of illusion and can therefore be ended. This liberation from all illusion is the essence of the spiritual quest.

SCIENCE AND RELIGION

If we consider religion to be belief, then it has no scientific basis, since it is personal and not a universal truth. But if we regard the essence of religion to be the ending of illusion, then it is a quest for discovering what is true and what is false. One could also call it unlearning the false through direct perception or insight. A mind that is freed of all illusion perceives 'what is' without any distortion and therefore its perceptions are as objective and universal as those in science. Science and spirituality then become two complimentary quests for discovering reality and there is no contradiction between them. Science is the quest for discovering the order that manifests in the world of space, time, matter and energy and religion becomes the quest for discovering order in consciousness (through the ending of illusion).

All great discoveries, even in science, have been the result of such creative insights beyond the known. How does the human mind discover something totally new which was never known before? The unknown is beyond thought and knowledge (memory). The human consciousness has this capacity for perceiving something beyond the known by making a foray into the unknown and such insights have led to great paradigm shifts (Kuhn, R. 1962) even in science. This is what distinguishes us from computers which have no awareness and therefore no capacity for insight.

Ramanujan (Kanigel, R. 1991) often 'saw' answers to questions in mathematics without knowing the proof. Einstein perceived the truths of relativity before he proved them mathematically, and Beethoven said, "I do not think out my music". How such perceptions come into consciousness is a great mystery.

EXTRA-SENSORY PERCEPTIONS

Since the human consciousness is capable of objective extra-sensory perceptions, these have sometimes led to unusual discoveries which now seem to be corroborated by scientific investigations. Some examples of these are cited below:

(i) *The Age of the Universe/Earth* (Blavatsky, H.P. 1988): In the ancient Hindu scriptures, the age of the universe/earth is divided into *yugas*, which occur cyclically, according to the following scheme:

Kritayuga (Stone Age)	1.728×10^6 years
Tretayuga (Bronze Age)	1.296×10^6 years
Dwaparyuga (Golden Age)	0.864×10^6 years
Kaliyuga (Iron Age)	0.432×10^6 years

Total = 1 Mahayuga = 4.320×10^6 years

It further says that 1000 such Mahayugas make 1 Kalpa which is one day in the life of Brahma, the creator. This means

1 Kalpa = 4.32×10^9 years

This value is very close to the present scientific value for the age of the earth which is 4.6×10^9 years and not too far from the present scientific value for the age of the universe which is about 13×10^9 years.

How did those ancient sages come to a figure which is at least of the same order of magnitude? Was it a myth or a perception?

(ii) *Occult Chemistry:* Mrs. Annie Besant and Mr. C.W. Leadbeater (Besant, A. and C.W. Leadbeater 1908) who were Theosophists working in Adyar, Madras, published a book in 1908 called *Occult Chemistry*, in which they wrote that they placed various minerals in front of them, made themselves smaller than the smallest particles in them and are writing what they actually 'see' as the structure within each element. They mentioned that those were 'records of observations' and not a product of their imagination.

The findings reported in this book have been compared with modern scientific knowledge about the structure of the nuclei in various elements and though they do not agree in entirety, there are uncanny parallels between them which have been documented by modern scientists: H.J. Arnikar (2000), S.M. Phillips (1980).

Apparently, there are other means of arriving at truths through extra-sensory perceptions which are not known to us in science. Indeed one of the great modern scientists named Schrödinger who founded Wave Mechanics, which was the precursor of modern Quantum Mechanics, studied the Vedas and commented that all thinking ended on the banks of the Ganges and modern science is merely re-discovering what those sages already knew ! This may be an exaggeration but it is perhaps not without some grain of truth in it.

(iii) *The Discovery of J. Krishnamurti* (Lutyens, M. 1975): In our own times, in the 20th century, Mr. C.W. Leadbeater 'saw' an unusual aura (a combination of colours around the brain) of a poor, young, emaciated 13-year-old boy named Krishnamurti while he was playing on the sea beach in Madras. From this observation, he predicted that this boy has an extremely rare aura with almost no trace of selfishness in it. He predicted that this boy will become a World Teacher. The boy was adopted by Mrs. Besant and brought up in the Theosophical Society. Though the boy was dull and could not pass any examinations, they never changed their mind. The boy later left the Theosophical Society, but he did become a World Teacher. The Buddhists choose a new Dalai Lama in the same way, by locating a boy with a highly developed spiritual consciousness.

Is this based on myth or on perception?

(iv) *Ayurvedic Herbs and Acupuncture:* How did the ancient sages in India discover the effect of various Ayurvedic herbs and how did those in China discover Acupuncture? The efficacy of both these is now tested scientifically but the sages did not use scientific double-blind experiments or trial-and-error to make these discoveries. Were these based on myth or perception?

CONCLUSION

Insights such as these do need to be tested by scientific methods, since they can get mixed up with subjective elements in the consciousness, such as desires, ambitions or dreams. But pure insights are perceptions of facts beyond the known and do occur in science, in art, in spirituality and they can be as pure and objective as scientific observations.

REFERENCES

Arnikar, H.J., 2000, *Essentials of Occult Chemistry and Modern Science*, Theosophical Publishing House, Chennai.

Besant, A. and C.W. Leadbeater, 1908, *Occult Chemistry*, Theosophical Publishing House, Chennai.

Blavatsky, H.P., 1988, *The Secret Doctrine...*, Theosophical Publishing House, Chennai.

Kanigel, R., 1991, *The Man Who Knew Infinity*, Scribners, London.

Kuhn, T., 1962, *The Structure of Scientific Revolutions*, University of Chicago Press.

Mary Lutyens, M., 1975, *Krishnamurti: The Years of Awakening*, Avon, New York.

Phillips, S.M., 1980, *Extra-Sensory Perception of Quarks*, Theosophical Publishing House, Wheaton, Illinois.

Weinberg, S., 1977, *The First Three Minutes*, Bantam Books.

4

Myths and Scientific Method

T.V. Ramakrishnan

I am completely out of place in this gathering. I am a physicist, hopefully working, with no experience or knowledge beyond his narrow area of specialization. I am remined repeatedly of the famous verse at the beginning of Kalidasa's *Raghuvansa* ...

"क्व सूर्यप्रभवो वंशः क्व चाल्पविषया मतिः।
तितीर्षुर्दुस्त्ररं मोहादुडुपेनास्मि सागरम्।।"

From this 'vantage point', I will extrapolate into large and vital areas of my ignorance.

My experience as a theoretical condensed matter physicist suggests the following. Our attempts have to do with nature as presented to us in controlled experiments, in various phenonmena, and increasingly, through observations in systems not natural but human-made. Indeed, the Royal Society of London, one of the earliest and perhaps the most influential body of scientists in the world, has as its motto 'nullius in verba' or 'not in (or by) words'. We also try to describe this understanding. Theory provides a language and a scheme for describing these observations and this understanding. In turn, the experiments we do, the phenomena we regard as significant, the systems made and what is studied in them, all depend on our view of the world, which is a construction of the mind, which thus depends on the theory. Briefly, the questions we ask, as Eistein said, depend on the theory ! The connection between experiment phenomena and theory as well as their relative weight is not often spelt out or rigid; it varies from subject to subject in science, varies in the same subject from one speciality to another, and even there, from time to time. For example, in the life sciences, experiment and phenomena are overwhelmingly predominant, while in some part of physics, theoretical argumentation.

There is of course the method of acquiring, verifying and solidifying this knowledge. The method called the 'scientific' method is hard; most of us spend our lifetime acquiring it and using it, and identifying it with science. Even this is not new. The great mathematician and geometrician, Euclid, when asked by the Pharaoh to teach his son geometry in an 'easy' way is reported to have said ... there is no royal road to geometry. But, it seems to me that science is more, much more. It is a continuing two-way interrogation of nature using methods and tools many of which arise in the process ! Another feature, greatly emphasized by sociologists of science, is the actuality or 'relativity' of science as practised by human beings conditioned by their experience and exposure, as social animals who are part of the increasingly powerful contract between the powers that govern, and economic forces that often drive and sustain this government. This gives to science the character of a powerful establishment and not of a dialogue with and description of nature with many resulting benefits for mankind (or the reverse, namely the search for human benefits being the source of better understanding of nature's workings).

One other characteristic of science I have noticed is that it works from inside out; there are no predetermined boundaries, no overarching 'philosophy' arrived at after pure thinking and anlysis which consciously determines the course of scientific work. Further, though science is often identified with reductionism and the method of reducing things to its components or elements is what all of us scientists work with every day, the phenomenon of emergence is too striking and prevalent in nature to be ignored. In my own field of work, namely condensed matter physics, perhaps the most spectacular phenomenon is superconductivity, or the complete absence of resistance to the flow of electrical current in a metal below a certain (low) temperature T_c, while just above that temperature, the same material has a non-zero electrical resistance. Nothing changes materially as you cross T_c, but the thing becomes perfect conductor. This is a real scientific phenomenon, discovered about a hundred years ago. It took nearly five decades (with failed efforts by many of the legendary names in science) before an atomic theory was proposed, with novel predictions which were verified later experimentally. This field is a good example of emergence; superconductivity does not reside in the individual atoms or molecules of the superconducting material and does not make sense for them; but *emerges* when they are put together. It is of course true that there is nothing in the constituents that *forbids* such a behaviour; nor is there a pointed indication. The microscopic or atomic laws are consistent with this 'collective' behaviour, they do not demand it. The rallying cry is 'More is different'. The effort of physicists in this and similar situations has been to identify the precise collective property or emergent behaviour displayed, and to describe it in terms of atomic 'elements' and their interactions. A more recent example is the realization that the number of 'expressed' proteins in the human body is more than the number of genes in the human genetic code. This implies that the well-known (and experimentally tested) dogma of 'one gene, one protein' is not fully right; collective efforts involving the manner in which the genes are spatially arranged, their interactions, etc., are importantly connected with proteins.

What is the relevance of all this to be matter at hand, namely myth and scientific studies? Very generally, I have the following impression. The hold of 'theory' in the humanities, in narrative subjects such as art, archaeology, sociology, economics ... is even stronger than in science. It also seems to me that the 'theory' is either often highly phenomenological or even epiphenomological, namely that it takes its task to be description of things as they seem to be; these scenes are taken to be the reality which needs to be distilled into an essence, the theory. This seems to me to be very superficial, almost supercilious. Either there is only one reality, namely the phenomenal/material experimental world 'organised' and described by science, or there in another underlying reality, popularly labelld mystical, but experienced and described similarly across centuries and across continents. Generally, from this perspective, the phenomenal/ material world is said to be 'māyic', to lack fundamental reality. If so, we (all beings) live and breathe in such a world—scientists try to decipher this world within itself. Some not well-answered questions are—Is consciousness an 'emergent' property? Does myth emerge out of consciousness and language? How?

The persistence and prevalence of myths is a clear indication of a reality different from that believed in by us scientists, and of our attempts to apprehend it. Since these myths have a material counterpart (stone and temples, words and books...) it is essential to use the 'scientific' method to solidify it. However, it may often happen that this bridging nature of myths (bridging two kinds of experimental/experiential reality) is lost sight of. I will, therefore, like to conclude by saying that the only source of knowledge is ultimately experiment or experience, and the dominance of or identification of an aspect of human knowledge with 'theory' is not good for the health of even 'theory'. This should always be kept in sight, especially by those who build mental structures. Myths are the unique bridge between the two, in that they probably arise as incomplete expression of a 'large' or comprehensive worldview and the processes predominantly identified with science (whose worldview is perhaps narrower) are necessary for consolidating them.

5

Spiritual and Scientific Perspectives in Jain Mythology

Viney Jain

JAIN MYTHOLOGICAL LITERATURE

Jainism, one of the world's oldest religious traditions, is not based on divine revelation. The validity of the philosophy, doctrines and way of life propounded in Jainism is derived from the omniscience of *Jinas/Tirthankars*, the spiritual leaders and supreme teachers who, having conquered their attachments/aversions, desires and passions, earned finite knowledge and eternal bliss. Their knowledge and teachings, at the initial stage (pre-writing stage), were transmitted to their disciples, orally and from one to the next generation in *Guru-Shishya Parampara* (in the tradition of teacher-taught way of transmission). Since the oral tradition ran the risk of distortion, due to the fading of the memory, written records of the oral tradition were prepared around 3rd century BCE, when writing became prevalent in India, and many religious and administrative documents were converted into permanent records. Unfortunately, many of the original scriptures compiled on the discourses of Tirthankar Mahavir (24th and last *Tirthankar*), who is dated to 6th BCE are lost. Thus, the available Jain scriptures of today, written between 100 and 800 CE by great *Acharyas* (scholars), contain only a part of the knowledge imparted by the omniscient *Tirthankars*.

In accordance with their contents, these scriptures are classified broadly into four major expositions, called *Anuyogas—Pratham-anuyoga* (Biographies, pre-historical and historical); *Charn-anuyoga* (Ethics/Conduct); *Karana-anuyoga* (Structure and Function of the cosmos and its constituents), and *Dravya-anuyoga* (Philosophy and nature of reality). *Pratham-anuyoga* is important for the present theme, as it comprises Jain Pauranic literature, which narrates Jain mythology. The Spiritual Journey through various births of 63 *Shalaka Purush* (Torch-Bearer has Personages)—*Tirthankars* (24), *Chakravarties* (12), 9 *Narayans* (9), *Prati-Narayans*(9) and *Baldevas* (9),—forms subject matter of these mythological stories. *Chakravarties* were great emperors who, having conquered the world, renounced all possessions, and practised austerities and penance to attain enlightenment and became *Jinas*. The *Narayans, Prati-Narayans* and *Baldevas* were great heroic figures, destined to become *Jinas/Tirthankars* in their future births. The later two also fair in the narrations of great epics *Ramayana* and *Mahabharata*, treasures of Hindu mythology.

The legends and discourses in Jain Puranas are believed to be based on the expositions given by omniscient *Tirthankars* to satisfy queries of audience and disciples in the universal assembly (*Samavsharan*). It is stated that various questions concerning myriad of subjects such as the functioning of the universe, nature and destinies of living beings, suffering and happiness, conduct of householders and monks, path to liberation were asked in the *Samavsharan* of every *Tirthankar*, starting from Rishabhdev to Vardhman Mahavir. The replies given by the *Tirthankars* were recorded faithfully, as is mentioned in *Adi Purana*. Acharya Jinsen states that he has made a humble attempt to faithfully transcribe the discourses by Gautam Gandhar, the chief disciple and interpreter of Tirthankar Mahavir, when queries of King Srenik (Empror Bimbisara of Magadh) were explained and satisfied at the time of *Samavsharan*. It may therefore be held that the contents of Jain Puranas, which are based on the explanations and teachings of the Tirthankar Mahavir, are datable to around 6th century BCE. But, the written scriptures of Jains are of much later date.

Kalpasutra, which contains life stories of 24 *Tirthankars*, is the earliest available text, written by Acharya Bhadrabahu, is dated, for instance, to *c*. 4th century BCE. The Digambara text *Tiloyapannatti*, dealing primarily with the structure and functioning of the cosmos, written by the mathematician Yativrishabha, in the 5th century CE, is still later in date. While Puranas, the poetic compositions of ancient legends and knowledge, were composed subsequently, incorporating both the oral and written

Digambara and Svetambara traditions. Written in Sanskrit, Prakrit or Apabhransha languages, the Jain Puranas have played very significant role in shaping the beliefs, value systems, rituals, spiritual practices and lifestyles of Jains. Some of the important Jain Puranas are mentioned in Table 5.1.

Table 5.1. The Major Jain Puranas.

Author	Language		Date
Padma Purana	Ravisen	Sanskrit	650 CE
Harivansa Purana	Jinsen II	Sanskrit	783 CE
Adi Purana	Jinsen II	Sanskrit	783 CE
Uttara Purana	Gunabhadra	Sanskrit	879 CE
Maha Purana	Pushpadanta	Apabhransha	9th century
Trisastishalaka Purusha Charitra	Hemachandrasuri	Sanskrit	12th century

Most popular legends in Jain mythological literature are described by Jinsen in *Adi Purana* which narrates the events from lives and teachings of Rishabhdev, the first *Tirthankar* (of the present time cycle) and his son Chakravarti Bharat. The biographies of the other 23 *Tirthankars*, including the last three, namely Neminath, Parshwanatha and Vardhman Mahavir have formed the subject matter of *Uttara Purana,* written by Gunabhadra, a disciple of Jinsen. These two form source for several Puranas written subsequently, as their accounts essentially are based on the descriptions of *Adi Purana* and *Uttara Purana.*

The central themes of Jain Puranas are concerned with describing and explaining the crossing-over (*tirtha*) of the ocean of worldly life by *Tirthankars* through spiritual purification to achieve the ultimate goal of absolute knowledge, bliss and freedom (*moksha*). The activities, efforts, events and their consequences are described within the framework of *karma* doctrine (principle of causality) in relation to the prevailing physical (material, spatial-temporal) and social (religious, political and socio-cultural) environments. In this context, the texts present a holistic account of a host of interrelated subjects such as cosmology, geography, biographies, history, science, metaphysics, religious doctrines, social and ethical conduct, statecraft, *karma* dynamics, rebirth, rituals, spiritual practices and philosophy.

Presentation and discussion of the scientific and spiritual perspectives in Jain mythology is a huge and complex task. Therefore, to limit the scope of the present paper, I shall attempt only to outline the essential features of the relevant Jain concepts on the constituents (including the living and non-living substances), structure and function of the universe and the universal values and goals of life exemplified by *Tirthankars*. Special reference will be made to the spiritual journey of the 23rd *Tirthankar*, Parshwanatha, who was born in Varanasi about 3000 years ago and whose historicity is now well established.

CONSTITUENTS, STRUCTURE AND FUNCTIONING OF THE UNIVERSE

Description of the universe in Jain Puranas is elaborate and fascinating. Besides the earth, suns, moons and stars, heavens and hells are described in detail (see, for example, *Adi Purana*, chapters 3rd and 4th). With little objective evidence, some of it appears to be fanciful. However, the basic conceptual framework is relevant and deserves serious study. Essential and unique features are mentioned below.

DYNAMIC REALITY OF THE UNIVERSE

The universe is real and not an illusion. It is eternal and was not created by anyone, and will never end. Universe is ever-changing and getting transformed.

The universe contains substances (*dravya*) which exist (*sat*), have intrinsic attributes (*guna*) and can transform into different modes or forms (*paryaya*). Continued existence and persistence of the essential qualities through change of form is an important characteristic of a substance.

The universe is a dynamic reality, characterised by interactions between its constituent substances (*dravya*), it functions and evolves as a system governed by Natural Laws.

CONSTITUENTS OF THE UNIVERSE

The constituent substances of the Universe are infinite but can be broadly grouped into two categories—the *ajeeva* (non-Living), the *jeeva* (living).

THE NON-LIVING SUBSTANCES

The non-living substances are devoid of the quality of consciousness (*chetana*) and are classified further into 5 different and independent classes:

A. *Akash-astikaya* (Space)
B. *Kala* (Time)
C. *Pudgalastikaya* (Matter, which can associate and disassociate)

D. *Dharmastikaya* (Field permitting Motion)
E. *Adharmastikaya* (Field permitting Rest)

AKASH-ASTIKAYA (SPACE)

Astikaya is an entity that exists (*asti*) and has extension or body (*kaya*). Among the *astikayas*, material (*pudgala*) substances only are perceptible. It is noteworthy that Time is not considered as an *astikaya*.

Akash-astikaya or Space is an objective reality, it consists of 2 parts— Occupied-Space (*lokakash*), which provides accommodation to all the substances; and Unoccupied-Space (*alokakash*), which surrounds the Occupied-Space and is infinite.

Fields permitting motion (*dharmastikaya*) and rest (*adharmastikaya*) manifest in the Occupied-Space allowing movement and rest of living-beings and non-living materials. Space, though continuous, can be considered as divisible into parts, the smallest unit *(pradesha)*, being the space occupied by a *paramanu*. In Unoccupied-Space, motion and rest are not possible because of absence of the substances *dharma* and *adharma*.

THE SHAPE AND DIVISIONS OF THE OCCUPIED UNIVERSE

The volume of the Occupied-Space, its shape, sizes and characteristics of different regions have been described in great detail in the Puranas. Gist of its salient features may be important to note. The Occupied-Space of the universe has a shape similar to a standing human figure and can be divided in three main regions (*Triloka*) as shown schematically in Fig. 5.1: (i) The Upper region (*Urdhvaloka*), the region of pleasure or heavens, where the celestial beings reside; (ii) The Middle region (*Madhyaloka*), the region of pleasure and pain and abode of lower celestial beings, humans, animals and plants and (iii) The Lower region (*Adholoka*), the region of increasing pain or hell, where living-beings are born to suffer due to their bad *karma* (actions) and passions in the past.

The middle world consists of concentric rings of continents, oceans and innumerable islands. Humans and animals exist in two and half continents (*Adhai-dvipa*) comprising *Jambu-dvipa* at the centre, surrounded by a salty ocean (*Lavana-samudra*), Dhaataki continent encircled by Kaalodadhi ocean and half of Pushkarvar continent. Several mountain ranges and rivers divide *Jambu-dvipa* in 7 different regions (*kshetra*);

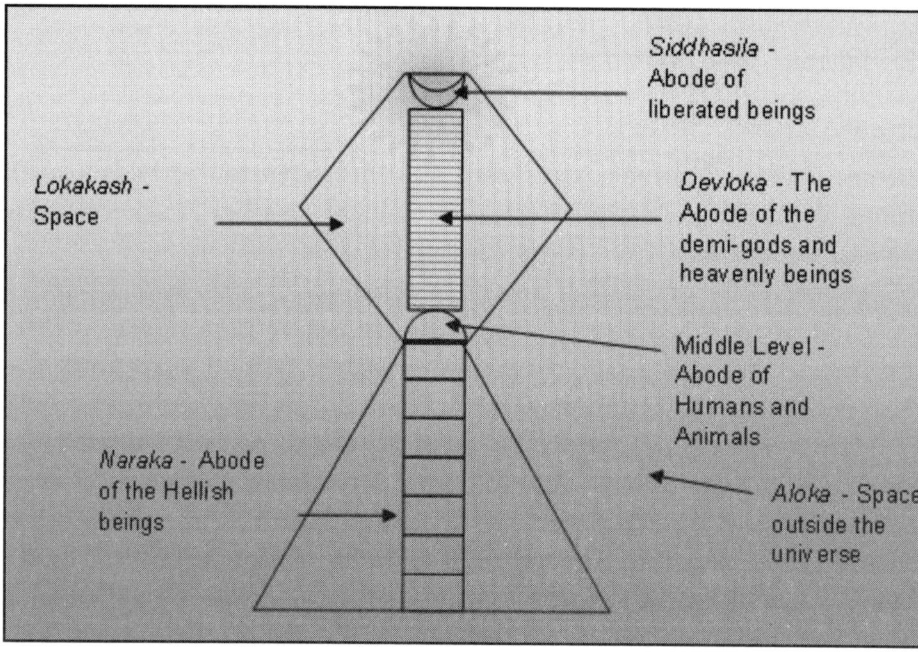

Fig. 5.1. Schematic Representation of the Structure of the Universe Described in Jain Mythology.
Source: Wikipedia.

southernmost is called Bharata, where we live; northernmost is Airavata similar in size and shape to Bharata and in the centre is located Maha-videha. Dhaataki and Pushkarvar continents each have two regions of Bharata, Airavata and Videha *kshetras*. Thus, there are 5 Bharata, 5 Airavata and 5 Videha regions in the two and half continents, where the worldly souls exist, evolve and transmigrate in forms of humans or animals. These regions constitute the *karma-bhumi* or lands of action where living-beings have to make efforts to fulfil their needs and desires in accordance with the universal laws such as the principle of causality or the *karma*-doctrine.

The areas of *karma-bhumi* are of special interest because it is only in *karma-bhumi* that the *Tirthankars* are born and guide the living beings on the path of spiritual evolution to attain liberation. All the other remaining parts of the *Madhyaloka* including 4 regions of Jambu continent, namely Hemavat, Harivarsh, Ramyak, Hirnayavat and 2 parts of Maha-Videha (Devkuru and Uttarkuru) are called lands of pleasure (*Bhog-bhumi*), since the needs and desires of the inhabitants in these lands are satisfied without effort by wish-fulfilling trees (*Kalpavriksha*).

There is little scientific evidence in support of the detailed physical structures of the universe as described in the Jain Puranas, however, views on cosmography continue to influence the Jain way of life even today. This may be because essentially the concept of the universe presented is that of a dynamic, interdependent and interactive system, uncreated and indestructible, which is rational and could be scientifically acceptable.

Time and Time-Cycle (*Kala Chakra*)

Time (*kala*) is an independent substance that manifests as an auxiliary cause to enable change. Time also has many modes and can change from one mode to another like other substances. Time has been described from two aspects: Real or Absolute (*nishchaya*) time and Apparent (*Vyavaharik*) or Empirically Measurable time (also called *samaya*).

Real time is divided into discrete units, (*kālānūs*), which exist, but have no extendable dimensions and do not form aggregates. Each point of space (*pradesha*) is associated with its own time point (*kālānū*) eternally functioning for it. One and the same *kālānū* represents the past with regard to the particles which have passed through it, present for those passing through it now, and future for those that will do so afterwards.

Apparent time (*samaya*) can be measured with the help of changing external factors such as movements of sun and moon and can be divided into eras, years, months, days, hours and so on. For example, in Bharata and Airavata regions of *Jambu-dvipa,* empirical time on a larger scale is manifested as a cycling wheel with ascending (*utsarpini*) and descending (*avasarpini*) arcs of equal duration. In the *utsarpini* arc, there is a gradual improvement in environment favouring spiritual evolution and enhancement of happiness, whereas in contrast to it the *avasarpini* arc is a slow decline in spiritual progress and wellness leading eventually to deteriorating environmental conditions.

Each half time-cycle is divided in 6 epochs of varying durations characterised in terms of degrees of suffering (*dushma*) and happiness (*sushma*). The first *Tirthankar*, Rishabhdev, was born in Bharata *kshetra* of *Jambu-dvipa* towards the end of the 3rd epoch (*sushma-dushma*) and other 23 *Tirthankars* in the 4th epoch (*dushma-sushma*).

At present we are in the 5th epoch, *dushma,* of *avasarpini,* characterised by increasing suffering. It is deemed to have begun a few years after the *nirvana* of Mahavira in 524 BCE and will last for 21000 years. It will be followed by the 6th epoch called *dushma-dushma* of increasing misery and worsening environment further for another

21000 years. After this period, the descending arc will end and again the first epoch of the ascending arc will gradually begin. The two arcs joined together make one cycle (*kalpa),* the *kalpa*s go on repeating forever and the universe goes on without end.

Interestingly, in the Videha regions of the *karma-bhumi* of the two and half continents, time manifests in a non-cycling mode so that the conditions in these regions always remain generally stable and conducive for spiritual progress, similar to the 4th epoch (*dushma-sushma*) of the descending cycle on our planet earth in *Jambu-dvipa.* Therefore, a rebirth in the regions of Videha presents an eternal opportunity to aspiring humans to attain the state of *Jina* or *Tirthankar* and achieve liberation. Present *Tirthankar* in Maha-videha region of *Jambu-dvipa* is Shri Simandhar Swami, who is also worshipped by Jains.

PUDGALASTIKAYA (*MATTER AND ENERGY*)

Matter is the only substance with a concrete or tangible form (*murta*). The term *Pudgalastikaya* denoting matter and energy is composed of 4 parts signifying its major characteristics: *puda* (association) + *gala* (dissociation)+ *asti* (existence)+ *kaya* (body). Thus, the most perceptible constituent of the universe, matter is a substance whose components have the unique quality of fusion/association and fission/dissociation.

The smallest non-divisible units of matter is called a *parmanu.* Each *parmanu* occupies one point of space (*pradesah*), and is a very subtle (*sukshma*) entity without mass (*agurulaghu*) and definite form. Thus, it remains unobserved by sense organs. A *parmanu* is, therefore, indivisible, indestructible and imperceptible ultimate particle of matter.

Two or more *parmanus* or ultimate particles can form different types of bonds and associate into aggregates, termed as *skandhas. Skandhas* have observable characteristics, such as touch, taste, smell and colour. Aggregates are classified according to size. Gross (*sthula*) aggregates are perceptible, and can be dissociated into smaller (*sukshma*) ones. In this way, the ultimate particles and aggregates of matter get transformed into innumerable modes (*paryayas*) and forms which constitute the manifold physically observed objects in the universe. Matter in a particular form or mode can remain in that form for the duration of the smallest unit of time (*samaya)* to innumerable units of time.

A unique feature of Jain philosophy narrated elaborately in the Puranas is the karmic-particles or the *karmons* which are special types of very subtle material *parmanus* permeating the entire occupied space. The *karmons* get activated in response to the mental and physical activities of living-brings and have the special ability to bind to the soul, thereby influencing the state of consciousness and future activities and destinies of the living-beings.

LIVING-BEINGS (*JEEVA*)

Jeeva, also called *Atma* (Soul), is an independent substance/entity, which is eternal and formless and is characterised by unique attributes of consciousness (*Chaitanya*) and bliss (*Ananda*). *Jeevas* are further classified into *Mukta* (Liberated souls) and *Sansarik Jeeva* (Worldly souls).

Liberated souls are perfectly pure souls (*Siddha*) which always reside at the top of the occupied universe and are characterised by infinite perception, knowledge, energy and bliss.

Worldly souls or embodied souls are those which are bonded with different forms of matter (*pudgala*) in subtle and gross physical bodies and are subjected to cycles of birth, death and rebirth into new bodies. The subtle bodies result from aggregates of very small, imperceptible, material particles, the *karmons*, forming a material karmic-body, which is always associated with radiant energy termed *Taijasa*-body.

Worldly souls are further classified into the following two:

(i) Immobile (*sthavara*) beings, whose bodies have only one physical sense, viz. sense of touch such as plants and,

(ii) Mobile (*trasa*) such as animals (*tiryancha*), humans (*manushya*), heavenly beings (*deva*) and hellish beings (*narki*). These are further categorised according to the physical bodies, they assume and the number of physical senses (two to five) they possess to interact with their environment. The five sensed beings have been sub-divided into those with mind and without mind.

Worldly souls transmigrate after death into any of these types determined by the state of their karmic-bodies.

The conscious attributes of pure soul get severely restricted (though not completely) and distorted by the karmic-body enveloping the soul. The observable differences between the forms and functions of the living beings are due to the diversity of the karmic material attached to the soul. The complex dynamics of interactions between the Soul and Matter determine the functions/behaviour and evolution of the living-beings.

Every worldly soul has the potential, in principle, to purify the self and evolve to the enlightened state of omniscience and subsequently achieve Liberation by completely dissolving the karmic-body. The path to achieve this goal of life is shown through biographies of the *Tirthankars,* so beautifully described in the Puranas.

The Dynamics of the Karmic-body in Relation to the Activities of the Physical Body

Every physical or mental activity by the living-beings produces some imperceptible effects besides perceptible consequences. The imperceptible effects have the potential of restricting and distorting the attributes of the soul/consciousness. These alterations in the consciousness are bought out by the bondage of the soul to the very subtle imperceptible particles of matter called karmic particles or *karmons.*

As mentioned earlier, the behaviour and evolution of living beings, in various physical forms, are essentially determined by the complex dynamics of interactions of the subtle, invisible, karmic-body with the soul and the gross physical body as shown schematically in Fig. 5.2.

Leshya (meaning: radiation/light) provides the link between the subtle- and gross-bodies. *Leshya* is defined as *bhava-dhara* (stream of psychic expressions), it links the invisible subtle-body with the gross physical-body and reflects the inner personality of the living-system.

Bhava-leshya, associated with the soul vibrations, expresses the state of consciousness. *Bhava-leshya*-induced activities of the physical-body (*yoga*) combined with passions (*kashaya*) enable *karma*-influx and bondage, which again affects the state of consciousness. *Dravya-leshya,* the material form is associated with the structure and function of the physical body. Thus, *bhava-leshya* and *dravya-leshya* determine behaviour dispositions.

Karmons have been classified, with respect to their effects on the psyche or the body, into 8 following major groups:

(i) Knowledge-Obscuring *karma* (*jnanaverniya*)
(ii) Perception-Obscuring *karma* (*darshanaverniya*)
(iii) Deluding *karma* (*mohiniya*)
(iv) Power-Obstructing *karma (antaraya)*
(v) Lifespan-Determining *karma* (*ayush*)
(vi) Physique-Determining *karma* (*naam*)
(vii) Status-Determining *karma* (*gotra*)
(viii) Feeling-Producing *karma* (*vediniya*)

First four types of *karmons* are considered harmful (*ghatiya*) since they directly obscure the expression of the basic characteristics of the soul; their complete elimination leads to omniscience. The last four types of *karma* are termed non-destructive (*aghatiya*) as they mainly affect the physical and social environments of the psyche. The Deluding *karma* (*mohiniya*) manifests as expressions of love and hate, while pain and pleasure are the result of the Feeling-Producing *karma* (*vediniya*).

Karma-dynamics is determined by the influx (*ashrava*) of *karmons*, their bondage (*bandh*) with the soul and dissolution (*nirjara*). The influx and bondage are mainly caused by the mental, vocal and physical activities of the living-being and its passions (such as anger, pride, deceit, greed). The bondage is determined by the nature and number of *karmons*, as well as the strength and duration of the bonds. The dissolution of the karmic-bondage occurs as a natural process of shedding after activation and completion of the bond duration. The process of dissolution can also be induced by spiritual practices like

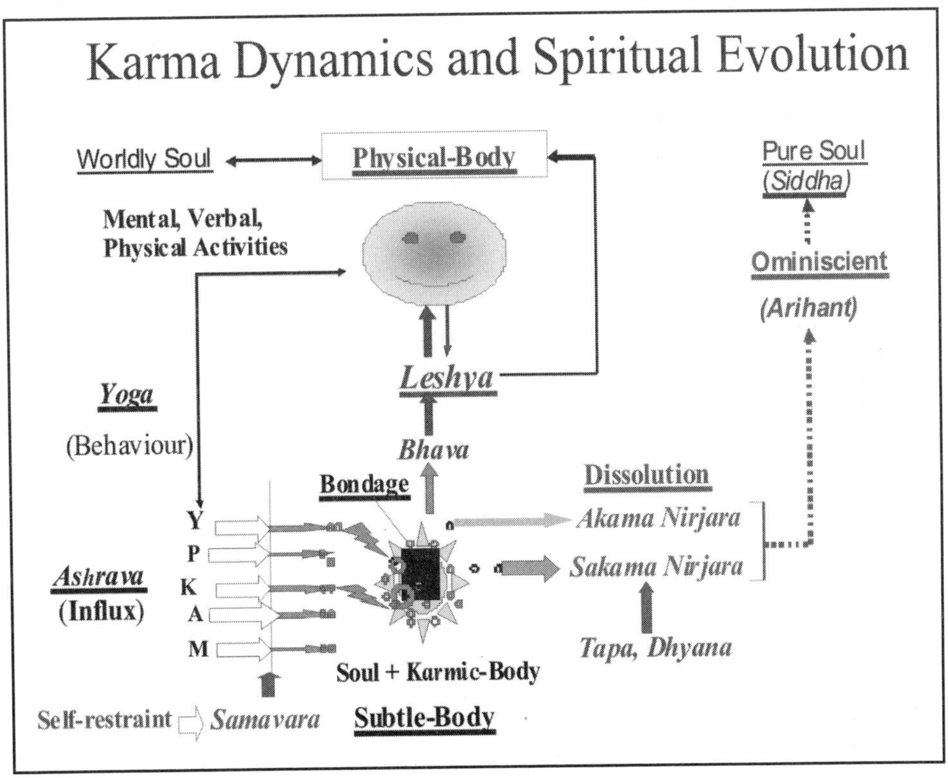

Fig. 5.2. *Karma* Dynamics and Spiritual Evolution to Omniscience and Liberation.

introspection (*pratikramana*), penance (*tapa*) and meditation (*dhyana*). The influx of *karmons* can be reduced by practice of self-restraint (*sanyama*). If the rate of dissolution of *karmas* exceeds the rate of influx, self-purification progresses through the reduction of the karmic-body. With the elimination of all *karmons* from the soul, the worldly soul becomes pure and gets liberated. The *karma*-dynamics and its effects on the spiritual evolution are depicted schematically in Fig. 5.2.

'TIRTHANKAR' IN JAIN MYTHOLOGY

To fully appreciate the significance of the spiritual and scientific aspects of the Pauranic literature, we need to understand the concept and the role of *Tirthankars* in Jainism.

Two categories of Enlightened Beings have been mentioned as follows:

- *Arhat/Arihant/Jina/Tirthankar* (Omniscient Soul with a Body)
- *Siddha* (Liberated 'Formless' Pure Soul)

An *Arhat* (worthy of devotion/reverence), having realised the true nature of the Self, is endowed with infinite knowledge and bliss, is free from all defects, passions, attachments and aversions, is destined to attain *nirvana* and become a *Siddha* after completing his lifespan (*ayush-karma*). Any Being (*Jeeva*) may, by its own spiritual efforts, become an *Arhat*, also called *Arihant* (one who has destroyed all his enemies, viz. *karmas*, passions etc.) or *Jina* (the victorious one), or *Kevalin* (omniscient).

> The name *Tirthankar* is derived from *tirtha*, meaning a place to cross-over (from the root R, meaning 'to cross'); Tirthankar (translated in English as Ford-Maker) is one who enables the crossing-over. A Tirthankar, besides being an Arhat, is also a Passionless (*Veetraagi*) Omniscient Spiritual Teacher and Benefactor, who shows the path to Liberation, Omniscience and Bliss to Every Living Being.

The status of *Tirthankar* is endowed with several special attributes and serves unique social/spiritual goals. The teachings of a *Tirthankar* provide rational explanations and help to understand the web of happenings in the universe mediated by diverse relationships and experiences of living beings. The teachings enlighten the seekers and inspire them to a righteous way of life leading to well-being, peace and ultimately to the goal of liberation.

The *Tirthankars/Jinas* are the ideal icons to be emulated. The lives of *Tirthankars* provide examples of highest spiritual evolution, which, in principle, can be achieved by every living-being. *Tirthankars* fulfil exemplary social roles in facilitating individuals and the society to evolve and develop fully their spiritual potentials. Therefore, *Tirthankars* are held in high esteem and have been accorded a very high status in Jain mythology.

Since ancient times the idols of *Tirthankars* are revered and worshipped with great devotion in Jain temples. This worship by the devotee is not for asking any favours but they adore the supreme qualities of *Tirthankars* as ideals to be emulated, thus reminding and inspiring oneself to achieve the desired goal of enlightenment by realizing the true nature of the Self. The *Tirthankar* represents the divinity in living-beings yet he is not a God in the sense of a creator and protector. He also cannot grant any favours, since he is completely unattached (*Veetraagi*) to the worldly affairs though endowed with infinite knowledge. He is a perfect Knower (*Gyata*) and Seer (*Drashta*) but not a Doer (*Karta*). The devotee can benefit only through his own motivations and efforts (*purushartha*) to follow the path shown by the *Tirthankar* and not by grace granted to him.

The status of *Tirthankar* is gained through a progressive process of realizing the potential of the Self through right attitude, knowledge and conduct for the welfare of all living-beings during a series of incarnations. Specifically, practices of sixteen *Karana Bhavanas* to inculcate the right attitudes and motivations in the previous birth lead to the incarnation of a *Tirthankar* (*Maha Purana*). We mention here, by way of example, only two of the most important of these *Bhavanas*, which include *Darshan Vishuddhi Bhavana* and *Vatsalya Bhava*.

The important components of *Darshan Vishuddai Bhavana* are:

Purification of Thoughts

- Development of passionless, equanimous and rational attitude (*Veetragata*).
- Knowing and believing substances as they are and not as they appear (Right Belief—*Samyakthva*).
- Holistic Thinking.

It is interesting to note that this is very similar to the attitudes required of a modern scientist, who objectively aspires to find the Truth by unbiased observations, experimentation and reason!

Vatsalya Bhava is practised to promote Wellness of All Living-Beings with

- Equanimity
- Humility
- Service and Compassion without Selfish Motives and Attachment

It is noteworthy that this is also the ideal of 'Social Responsibility and Ethics in Science'.

Thus, the practice of *Darshan Vishuddhi Bhavana* and *Vatsalya Bhava* also endow the *Tirthankar* with the qualities required of a socially responsible scientist *par excellence.*

Auspicious Events in the Life of A Tirthankar

There have been 24 *Tirthankars* during the current time-cycle; Rishabhdev was the first and Vardhman Mahavir the last. Pauranic Literature describes five auspicious events (*Panch-Kalyanak*) in the life of every *Tirthankar* celebrated for the wellness of all living beings:

- *Garbha* (conception) *Kalyanak*: 16 auspicious dreams of the Mother, signifying the event of conception of a great personage.
- *Janma* (Birth) *Kalyanak*: Birth, *Abhisheka,* celebrations and Naming ceremonies by Indra.
- *Diksha* (Initiation) *Kalaynak*: Renunciation of worldly life, adoption of the life of an ascetic, initiation of austerities and spiritual practices for self-purification, observing silence during the period
- *Jnana Kalyanak*: Enlightenment and Omniscience (*Kaivalya Jnana*). A *Tirthankar*, after attaining omniscience, enlightens the fellow living-beings by his discourses. A special pavilion, called *Samavasharan* is created for the discourses and sermons (*Divya Dhwani*), which are attended by all categories of humans, gods and animals. Questions/ queries from the audience are answered by the *Tirthankars* and his chief disciples (*Gandhars*).
- *Moksha Kalyanak*: Liberation, freedom from body/matter, ascends to *Siddhashila*.

Tirthankar Parshwanatha: Quasi–Mythological Account of his Spiritual Journey

Studies concerning Parshwanatha are important because of his great popularity and the significant socio-cultural impact of his life and teachings lasting till the present day (Jain, Sagarmal; 1988). Historicity of Parshwanatha, based on several literary references in Jain and Buddhist scriptures, is well accepted by scholars of Indology (Jacobi 1884; Charpentier 1922; Radhakrishnan 1929; Majumdar, 1946; Jain 1988; Jain et al. 1999).

The basic facts about the parentage, birth, renunciation, enlightenment, teachings, death and liberation of Parshwanatha have been given in the ancient Jain scriptures such as *Rishibhashit, Kalpasutra,* and *Tiloyapannatti. Rishibhashit* is perhaps the oldest scripture (5th century BCE) written in Ardhamagadhi Prakrit, which discusses in a non-sectarian way the philosophies of 44 Indian *rishis* from several Vedic, Jain and Buddhist traditions. A separate chapter deals with Parshwanatha's ideas/ views on the universe, soul, *karma, moksha* and path to liberation (Jain, Sagarmal 1988).

It is noteworthy that the detailed biographical accounts of *Tirthankars* are generally lacking in the older scriptures (written between 3rd century BCE and 8th century CE), which focus mainly on the philosophies, doctrines, spiritual practices and ethics. A few variations, in the exact names of Parshwa's parents, in the *Kalpasutra* (Svetambar) and *Tiloyapannatti* (Digambar) texts have been pointed out. Notwithstanding the minor differences in the ancient texts, scholars generally agree on the following basic facts of Parshwa's life:

> Born in Varanasi, in 877 BCE, as a son of the King Ashwasen (Hiyasen/Vishwasen) and Queen Vama Devi (Vammila, Brahmi), Parshwanatha renounced the worldly life and adopted life of an ascetic at the age of 30 years. After rigorous meditation (*dhyana*) and penance (*tapa*) for 83 days, he attained Omniscience at Ahishetra (near Barelly, U.P.) and subsequently travelled widely to deliver philosophical and religious discourses at various places. For spiritual progress, he advocated the Four Dimensional Path (*Chaturyam Dharma*), emphasizing the practice of non-violence, truth, non-stealing and non-attachment to worldly things,. Parshwanatha died and attained *nirvana* at the age of 100 years from Samed Shikhar (Parasnath Hill, Dist. Hazaribag, Jharkhand).

Though the legends and events of his past lives narrated in Jain Puranas are unverifiable and can be considered as myths, yet these are inspiring for attaining the highest spiritual level and becoming of *Tirthankar*. Besides, there are several biographies, composed after the 8th century CE, and written in different languages like, Prakrit, Apabhransha, Sanskrit, Kannada, Gujarati and Hindi, which describe the events happening during ten spiritual evolutionary incarnations of Parshwanatha. More than 25 such biographies have been published. While most of these biographies agree on the basic facts of Parshwanatha's life, there are variations in the narration of the associated legends, which possibly originate from blending of the prevalent and popular oral versions with creative imagination of the authors. The list of important biographies along with their author, language and date are mentioned in Table 5.2.

Table 5.2. Major Biographies of Parshawanath.

Title of Text	Author	Date in Common Era	Language
Parshabhudaya	Jinsen	783	Sanskrit
Parshwanathacharit	Vadiraj Suri	869	Sanskrit
Pasanahchariu	Padmakirti	1077	Apabhransha
Pasanahchariu	Budh Sridhar	1132	Apabhransha
Parshwanathacharitra	Hemvijay	1575	Sanskrit
Parshwa Purana	Chandrakirti	1597	Sanskrit
Parshwa Purana	Bhudhar Das	1789	Hindi

MAJOR LEGENDS AND EVENTS OF THE LIFE OF PARSHWANATHA

Legend of the Hermit and Burning Snakes

Hermit Mahipala was performing *Panchagni Tapa*. Surrounded by burning fires all around, unmindful of causing injury to others, he was cutting firewood to add to the fires. Parshwanatha, endowed with clairvoyance, asked him to stop and exclaimed, "There dwell in that log a serpent couple, please do not hurt them".

The hermit did not believe him, got annoyed and did not stop, thereby cutting the snakes into pieces.

Prince Parshwa recited *Namokar Mantra* to the dying serpent couple.

Parshwanatha, who was then 30 years of age, felt very sad watching and reflecting on the sufferings of innocent beings, decided to renounce the world and adopted life of an ascetic.

Legend of Torture by Demon and Protection by Snake Gods

- The serpents were reborn in heaven as Deva Dharnendra and Devi Padmavati.
- Humiliated, the hermit dies and was born as a Demon God named Shambhar.
- While Parshwa was meditating on the nature of pure soul, Shambhar, remembering the events of past life, started to torture him to take revenge.
- Dharnendra and Padmavati, who were grateful to Parshwa, descended from heaven to offer protection against *upsarga* by the Demon Shambhar (Kamath).
- Parshwanatha, undisturbed by the torture, continued meditation and contemplation of the Pure Self, thereby attaining enlightenment and ominiscience (*kaivalya jnana*).

Jnana Kalyanak: Omniscience (Kaivalya Jnana) and Sermons in the Holy Assembly

A holy assembly called *Samavsharan* or the universal gathering of all categories of living-beings is established so that all beings can benefit from the religious and philosophical discourses of the Omniscient Parshwa. In order to offer this unique opportunity to a large number, the *Samavsharan* travels from place to place, through many regions. Inquisitive disciples/ visitors in the assembly paying homage to the *Tirthankar*, humbly request to be enlightened and seek answers to many pertinent and universal questions regarding the nature and happenings in the universe, the nature of *Jeeva* and path to liberation (Gunabhadra: *Uttara Purana*; Budha Sridhar: *Pasanahchariu*, chapters 9 and 10). For example:

- *Gandhara Svayambhu* asks Tirthankar Parshwanatha: "How is this Universe formed and functions?"
- King Prabhanjan wants to know about the nature of *Jeeva.*
- King Ravikirti asks about the conduct of a householder.

PREVIOUS LIVES OF PARSHWANATHA: VICTORY OF FORGIVENESS OVER MALICE, ANGER AND REVENGE

When the *Samavsharan* reaches Varanasi, parents of Parshwanatha, King Hiyasen and Queen Vamadevi, come to pay homage. King Hiyasen wishes to be enlightened about the purpose of human life. *Tirthankar* dwells upon the rarity of acquiring the human form by the *Jeeva* as a consequence of activation of auspicious *karma*. This is very valuable since liberation from the cycle of birth and death is possible only for the humans. Therefore, the worthwhile goal of human life is to evolve spiritually by developing rational (*samyak*) perception, knowledge and conduct.

Deva Dharnendra wants to know about the reasons underlying torture inflicted on Parshwa by Demon Shambhar. In response to the query of Dharnendra, Tirthankar Parshwanatha recounted the events of his past lives (chapters 11and 12, Budha Sridhar: *Pasanahchariu*), which are listed in Table 5.3.

Table 5.3. Summary of Successive Lives of Marubhuti and Kamath.

• *Marubhuti*	*Kamath,* Feels humiliated, revengeful, kills Marubhuti
• Elephant	Snake, Bites and kills
• Deva (Sahastrar heaven)	5th Hell
• Vidyadhar king	Python, Swallows
• Deva (Achyut heaven)	6th Hell
• Chakravarti	Bheel, Kills by Arrow
• Ahmindra (Greyavak heaven)	7th Hell
• King Anand	Lion, Attacks and Eats
• Indra (Aanat heaven)	4th Hell
• Tirthankar Parshwa	Demon Shambhar, Tortures and Repents

The reasons can be traced to Parshwa's tenth previous life when he was named Marubhuti, the son of a royal priest in the court of King Arvind, the ruler of Podanpur in Bharatkshetra of *Jambu-dvipa*. Shambhar was his elder brother named Kamath, a bad character, jealous, full of deceit and revenge. Marubhuti was simple, humble and forgiving. His father, being a religious and pious person, renounced the worldly life to become an ascetic. King Arvind appointed Marubhuti in his father's place ignoring the elder brother Kamath.

Kamath seduces the beautiful wife of his younger brother while Marubhuti was away on a mission with King Arvind. On learning about this on his return and verifying by his own eyes, Marubhuti, feeling very sad and angry, complains to the king, who punishes and orders Kamath to leave his kingdom.

After a few days, Marubhuti started missing his brother and was full of remorse considering himself responsible for his brother's misfortune and suffering. Marubhuti sets out in search of Kamath and finds him among a group of mendicants practising painful exercises and self-torture. Marubhuti asks for forgiveness for causing hurt and requests Kamath to return home. Kamath gets annoyed, picks up a rock and throws it on the head of Marubhuti, killing him instantly. King Arvind, on hearing the tragic news, became detached and, renouncing the worldly life, decided to lead the life of a monk.

Marubhuti was reborn as an elephant in a forest. Once, Muni Arvind was practising deep meditation in the same area. The elephant, on seeing the Muni meditating in Kayotsarga posture with the vision focused on the tip of the nose, became very calm and stood watching him. Muni Arvind opened his eyes and knowing through clairvoyance that the elephant standing before him was the reincarnation of Marubhuti, addressed him thus "O Elephant King, remember that you are the reincarnation of Marubhuti, the royal priest of Podanpur. Your elder brother had seduced your wife and murdered you. You are born as an elephant because you had unpleasant and sad feelings at the time of death. Now you should maintain pious intentions and practise self-restraint and good conduct so that you can rid of your inauspicious *karma* and get liberated". The elephant, remembering his past life, recognized the Muni as King Arvind, his master, and decided to follow his advice. After the departure of the Muni, the elephant indeed led a life of restraint, fasting, avoiding hurting anybody and being helpful to its fellow creatures.

One day, a fire broke in the forest. To save itself from fire, the elephant took shelter in a mud-pond. Kamath, after his death, was also born as a poisonous serpent in the same forest. On seeing the elephant, the serpent recognized it as the enemy responsible for humiliation in the previous birth. The serpent bit the elephant in revenge, who died peacefully tolerating the pain and was subsequently reborn as *Deva* in heaven. The serpent was reborn in the 5th hell.

The cycle of anger, revenge, hurt and violence from Kamath and tolerance and forgiveness without any malice or violence on the part of Marubhuti continued for a long time during several incarnations (summarised in Table 5.3). Due to his bad intentions and cruel deeds, Kamath had to suffer untold pain in hell, while Marubhuti, because of his virtuous intentions and auspicious *karma*, enjoyed the pleasures in heaven. Eventually, Kamath in the incarnation of demon Shambhar did realise his mistakes, repented and asked for forgiveness only after Marubhuti, reborn as Parshwanatha, attained omniscience (*kaivalya jnana*) by continuing deep meditation, undisturbed by tortures inflicted by Shambhar.

Important Spritual and Scientific Perspectives and Suggested Reasearch Topics

Manifold important spiritual lessons can be derived from the above mentioned quasi-mythological legends. For example, these stories vividly illustrate the operation of the universal laws of *karma* (causality) and *karma-phala* (consequences) which originate from the passions (anger, pride, love, hate and desires) and actions (violence, crime, etc.) of living-beings. The *karmas* of the past influence the physical and social behaviour of beings in the present and future births. The importance of efforts—to purify the Self through self-discipline, equanimity, renunciation, meditation and contemplation—and to realise the true nature of the Soul leading to transformation of *leshya* and higher levels of consciousness have been emphasized in the Pauranic literature (Fig. 5.2). Practices of self-restraint and virtuous meditation, in particular, have been recommended as effective methods for the stoppage of the karmic-influx/bondage and dissolution of the karmic-body leading to self- purification (*Adi Purana*, chapter 21).

Recent empirical researches have demonstrated significant benefits of meditation for behavioural modification, stress reduction and multiple health gains. It would be worthwhile, therefore, to undertake systematic and comprehensive research projects to further investigate the psycho-biological, neurological, genetic and epigenetic mechanisms/processes induced by self-restraint practices (such as fasting) and different meditative techniques in relation to transformation of *leshya* and spiritual evolution.

Supreme Forgiveness (Uttam Kshama)

The biography of Parshawanatha illustrates the significance of developing the disposition of instant, unconditional, universal and absolute forgiveness (*uttam kshama* or Supreme Forgiveness) for spiritual progress. Supreme forgiveness is believed to arise from the basic benevolent nature of the pure soul and does not depend in anyway on the extrinsic circumstances

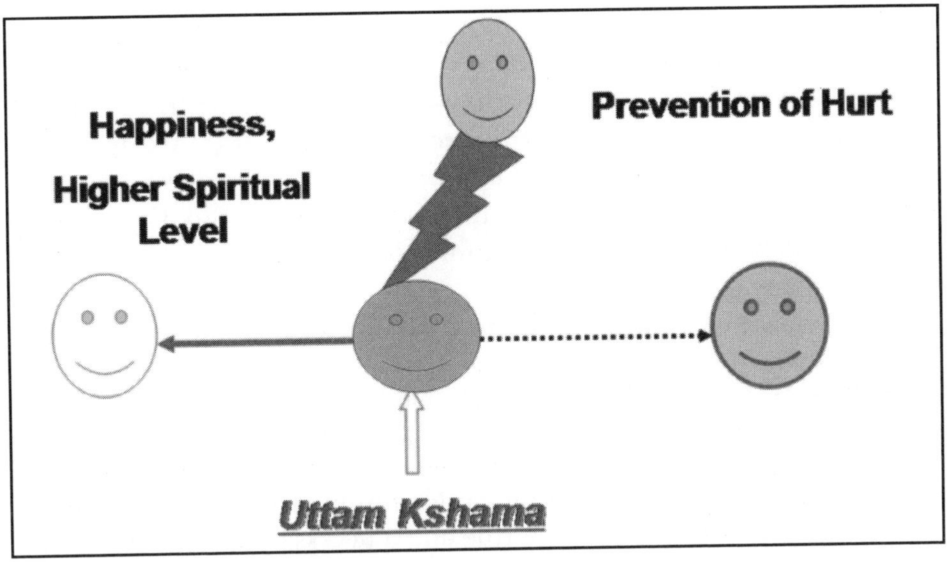

Fig. 5.3A. Effects of Supreme Forgiveness on Happiness and Spiritual Evolution.

such as expression of an apology and repentance from the offender or retributive punishment meted out to him. *Uttam kshama,* emerging from the pure, passionless state of equanimity of the Soul, is expressed spontaneously, unconditionally and universally.

Manifestations of *uttam kshama* in the worldly soul (*sansarik jeeva)* are, however, restricted or distorted due to the karmic bondage to the Soul. Rational vision and rational knowledge provide the essential basis for right conduct (*samyak charitra*) necessary for self-purification. Realization of the true nature of the Self is the only real pathway for the evolution of *uttam kshama.* A person having a psychic disposition for supreme forgiveness does not feel hurt by any offence, is not angry, has no desire for revenge and attains a higher Spiritual State enhancing peace and happiness (Fig. 5.3A). In contrast, a disposition that is deficient in the trait of forgiveness suffers in anger, vengeance and violence as demonstrated by the behaviour of Kamath.

Development of a disposition expressing high degree of forgiveness is very relevant to modern times where anger, hate, violence and terror are increasingly threatening the spiritual, mental and physical health at the personal level and sustainable socio-economic development and peace at the global level. Practising true forgiveness in real life is very difficult, however, despite all the teachings and awareness of potential benefits. Considering the practical aspects, it may appear that practising supreme forgiveness as conceived and propagated in Jain traditions is almost impossible. Is it then only a mythical concept emerging from the legends associated with the spiritual journey of Tirthankar Parshwanatha? In view of the relevance of this concept and its implications, comprehensive interdisciplinary theoretical and experimental research studies to explore enhancement of the disposition to forgive by spiritual practices such as virtuous meditation (*dharma dhyana*) are warranted to answer this query.

Forgiveness as a virtue has been emphasized by all the religions since ancient times. In Abrahamic religions (Judaism, Christianity and Islam), forgiveness is considered as divine gift (God's grace and kindness) that is often linked to the confession and repentance by the offender. In Buddhism, the concept of loving kindness (*metta*) emphasizing universal love and compassion implicitly includes forgiveness. Hindu scriptures describe forgiveness as a moral virtue and a necessary instrument for the preservation of life. Interest in secular research on forgiveness and associated benefits have been rather sparse until last few decades. Interestingly, after the terrorist attacks on 09.11.2001 on the World Trade Center in New York, there has been an explosion of empirical and theoretical multidisciplinary research on forgiveness, including psychobiological and psychosocial aspects.

From the viewpoint of modern psychology, forgiveness is conceptualized as a multidimensional construct that is formed by interplay between cognition, emotion and behaviour. It is considered as a complex act of consciousness that liberates the psyche and soul from the need for personal vengeance and the perception of the self as a victim.

For the evolutionary biologists, forgiveness is a basic trait common to many animal species. The capacity to forgive is a complex biological adaptation extending throughout the animal kingdom (Wilson 2002), which evolved as a regulatory mechanism to restore interpersonal relationships that provide survival advantage. The gene-based kin selection theories also suggest that individuals with benevolent attitudes sacrificing their self-interests for their group or for their relatives will be favoured by natural selection.

Initial studies to explore the genetic basis indicate that genetic polymorphism in the dopamine receptor gene correlates with dispositions of anger and forgiveness. Neuroimaging (fMRI) studies have suggested that specific brain regions such as frontal-limbic circuits may mediate processes involved in forgiveness (Stein and Kaminer 2006).

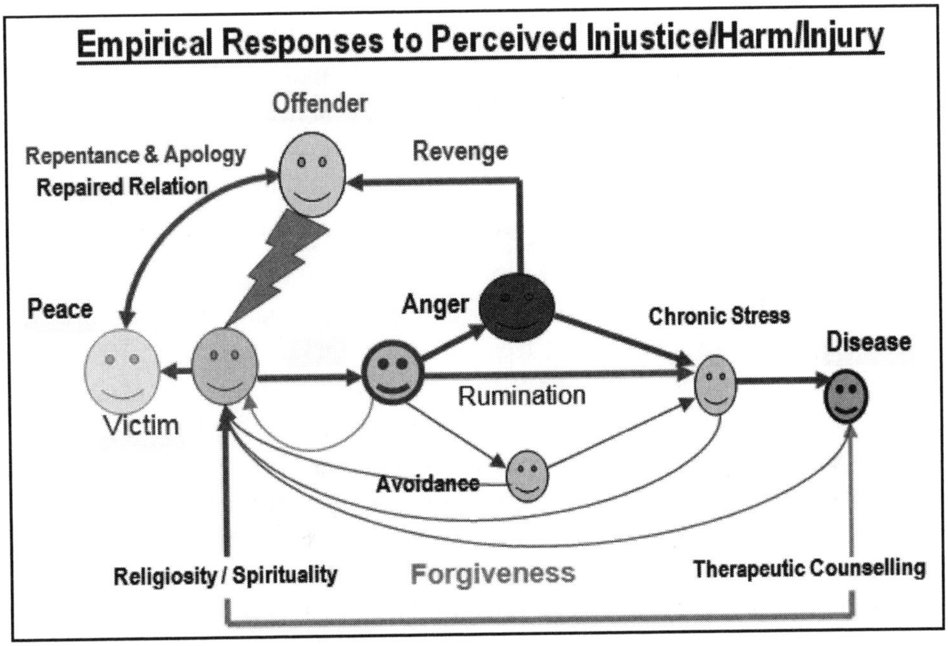

Fig. 5.3B. Simple Model Showing Prevention and Repair of Harm by Forgiveness.

Empirical studies conducted on a group of young college students in USA indicate that the prime motivations underlying forgiveness are self-oriented, like repairing an important relationship or preventing harmful stress. Inability to forgive has been shown to induce chronic stress and disease, whereas forgiveness enhances health by reducing psycho-social stress and fatigue, lowering blood pressure and lower-back pain, promoting immune responses, reducing anxiety, depression and psychopathology.

Based on empirical psychobiological research, possible responses to hurt caused by an offence and benefits (prevention of harm/distress/ disease) of choosing the path of forgiveness are schematically depicted in a simple model in Fig. 5.3B.

Studies suggesting a positive correlation between spirituality and forgiveness and a negative correlation between dispositional forgiveness and vengeance need to be confirmed and extended to groups from diverse socio-cultural and religious backgrounds.

A comparison between Figs. 5.3A and 5.3B illuminates the differences between the Ideal/ Transcendental view of supreme forgiveness and the empirical/pragmatic view.

Summary and Concluding Remarks

Jain Puranas, based on the knowledge imparted by the omniscient *Tirthankars* and composed with the blend of scholarship and creative imagination of great *acharyas* and poets, are rich sources for spiritual and scientific insights, which could be of great value in meeting the challenges of the 21st century. A few relevant viewpoints are highlighted below.

- The vision of the external Universe, presented in Jain mythology, appears in part—especially the cosmography elaborately describing the spatio-temporal structures for different heavens and hells and also the account of the middle world where humans and animals exist—as science fiction far removed from observable facts. However, it contains many attractive and interesting concepts and insights illustrated by the lives of the great personages and legends associated with them. Importantly, this mythical vision, viewed holistically from the conceptual and theoretical framework of *karma* doctrine (principle of causality) and rebirth operating via interactions of living and non-living substances, provides a rational explanation of the unfolding potential for spiritual evolution of all living-beings (*jeeva*) within the manifold diversity of the worldly happenings.
- The omniscience of the *Jinas/Tirthankars* is gained through enhancing the inherent intuitive processes of gaining right knowledge (without directly involving sensory perceptions) through eliminating passions and cultivating equanimity (*Veetragata*) by techniques of introspection, meditation and contemplation on the real nature of the Universe and the Self. This leads to higher levels of consciousness and spiritual purification. In contrast, the scientific methods of knowing the external world comprise sensory-perception-based observation, experimentation, verification and logical reasoning. Both the approaches complement each other.
- Pauranic expression of the belief that spiritual evolution leading to omniscience and liberation is possible only in human form and that too only from *karmabhumi* during the *sushma-dushma* epoch of the time-cycle is noteworthy. Among all the life forms, humans and animals are subjected to experience of both pleasure and pain; whereas, the heavenly beings are engrossed overwhelmingly in the hedonistic pursuits (enjoyment/pleasure) and hellish beings suffer from pain relentlessly. In the Bharatakshetra of *karmabhumi*, the abode

of humans and animals, pain and pleasure both are experienced by living-beings during the 3rd (*sushma-dushma*) and 4th (*dushma-sushma*) epochs of the time-cycle. However, spiritual progress leading to omniscience and liberation in Bharatakshetra is possible only during the 4th epoch, the time period of living *Kevalins* and *Tirthankars* described in the Jain mythology. The reasons for such a limitation are not clear. Does this signify that for spiritual evolution achieving higher levels of awareness, experience of a certain level of pain and suffering (constituting stress) are important? To clarify this question, relationships between suffering pain/stress, environment and spirituality need to be explored.

- Also relevant, in this context, are the descriptions of regions of Videhakshetra, where according to *Adi Purana* the cyclic mode of time does not operate and the events happen under stable environmental conditions, similar to the 4th epoch in Bharatakshetra persisting eternally, enabling both happiness and suffering. In this region, *Tirthankars* are continuously present inspiring and guiding the laypersons to lead a non-violent, ethical, self-restrained and eco-friendly way of life. People are healthy, humble, kind and do not hurt each other. Land is fertile, climate is benign and natural calamities are rare. The Videha region, thus, presents a model of balanced and sustained development with an environment conducive to spiritual evolution. Striving and meritorious living-beings may be reborn in Videhaksetra and can gain enlightenment and liberation. This unique mythical model of Videhakshetra is worthy of serious study in the context of the present risks of self-destruction posed by increasing environmental pollution, global warming, unlimited consumption, greed, crimes and violence promoted by the prevalent hedonistic and materialistic life-styles in our world.
- The legends associated with Tirthankar Parshwanatha described in Jain mythology suggest that development of supreme and absolute forgiveness (*uttam kshama*) by spiritual practices can help in achieving higher levels of consciousness, peace, happiness and liberation (shown schematically in Fig. 3A). Systematic and co-ordinated biophysical and psychobiological scientific studies using modern methodology to explore such possibilities are likely to facilitate integration of spiritual and scientific approaches and yield rich dividends.

REFERENCES

Charpentier, J., 1922, *Archives d'Etudes Orientales*, Vol. 18, Uppsala, p. 18.

Datta, O. Kinkar, 1946, *An Advanced History of India*, Macmillan, London.

Jain, Sagarmal, 1987, *Arhat Parshwa aur Unki Parampara*, Parshwanath Vidyashram, Varanasi.

Jain, Sagarmal, 1988, *Rishibhashit: A Study*, Prakrit Bharati Academy, Jaipur.

Jain, A.K., J.K. Jain and S.C. Jain (eds.), 1999, *TirthankarParshwanath*, Prachya Shraman Bharti, Muzaffarnagar.

Jinsen, Acharya, 1988, *Adi Purana*, Hindi Translation (ed. by Panna Lal Jain), Bharatiya Jnanpith, New Delhi.

Kalpasutra: Translated from Prakrit by H. Jacob, *Sacred Books of the East*, Vol. 45, Jain Sutras, Part II, Claredon Press.

Padamkirti: Pasanahcariu, Hindi Translation [P.K. Modi (ed.)], Prakrit Text Society, Varanasi, 1965.

Radhakrishnan, S., 1929, *Indian Philosophy*, Vol. 1, Muirhead Library of Philosophy (2nd edition), George Allen and Unwin Ltd., London.

Sakalakirti: Parshwanatha Charita, Hindi Translation [Pannalal Jain (ed.)], Bharatvarshiya Anekant Vidvat Parishad, Varanasi, 1998.

Shridhar, Budh, 2006, *Pasanah Chariu*, Hindi Translation [Raja Ram Jain (ed.)], Bharatiya Jnanpith, New Delhi.

Stein, D.J. and D. Kaminer, 2006, 'Forgiveness and Psychopathology, Psychobiological and Evolutionary Underpinnings', *CNS Spectr* 11(2): 87-89.

Wilson, D.S., 2002, 'Darwin's Cathedral: Evolution', *Religion and the Nature of Society*, University of Chicago Press, Chicago.

Case Studies

काशी दर्पण

6

Jataka Stories and Archaeology: A Case Study of Varanasi

Vidula Jayaswal

INTRODUCTION

Jatakas narrate stories of previous lives of Buddha. In each story Bodhisattva takes birth as member of different sections of the society. His portrayal as one or the other member of animal kingdom too occurs. The Jatakas, a rich section of Indian mythology, assume to mirror society and geo-physical environment of ancient times. But, the time of the narrated events or situations, and the compilation of the Jataka stories are quite apart from one and other. The concept of Jataka stories takes one much beyond the sphere of the presence of historical Buddha (6th century BCE). Because, these are stories of his many births through which he passed. But, the theme and compilation of the Jatakas in historical pursuit is organised between the time frame of *c*. 3rd century BCE and 4th century CE. The enquiry which comes to mind is, whether the events of these narrations have historicity? Also, is it possible to ascertain socio-physical environments of Jataka stories within a chronological frame? Answer to these enquiries would certainly enrich our understanding of Indian culture, which is strongly rooted in the past.

Since the time bracket ascertained for the compilation of the Jataka stories is broad, scientific evaluation of each of the incident or core theme

Fig. 6.1. View of exposed ritual floor of Sunga period, Aktha.

needs to be attempted individually. Study of material remains of the past, the focus of archaeology, brings forth comparable geo-cultural environments of some of these mythological stories. This exercise is expected to be beneficiary for both—archaeology and mythology. The former dealing primarily with the artefacts, has great quantum of data of material nature. Ideologies, concepts and conventions of the society in this case exist beneath thick cover of technology, craft, art and skills. Myths, vibrant in concept, idea and imagination, have been integral part of our culture for centuries together. Their long survival results in multi-layered cover of elaboration and alteration of the core theme. Thus, the correlation between the two—archaeology and Jatakas—though useful, is a challenging exercise. The present attempt is a case study to explore possibility to develop an interdisciplinary investigative programme for the study of myths and archaeology.

Varanasi fares well in the Jatakas. Historical format of ancient Varanasi too is well documented in archaeological records. Thus, the two provide good case study, which is based on correlation of comparable incidences of Jatakas and the excavated remains. The same is attempted in this paper. I have selected two Jatakas—*Akitta-Jataka* (No. 480) and

Fig. 6.2. Exposed floor of Sunga period, with traces of fire alters on a ritual platform, Aktha.

Kachhapa-Jataka (No. 178)—for this case study. The two narrate diverse socio-environmental facets of ancient Varanasi. Thereafter, another case study is proposed, in which a group of Jatakas has been included. Jatakas, like *Yuvanjaya* (No. 460), *Cullasutasoma* (No. 525), *Udaya* (No. 458), *Sonandana* (No. 532), and *Khandala* (No. 120), address Varanasi by different names. The chronological growth of settlement of Varanasi too is marked by shift of colonies of ancient period from one to the other areas. The archaeological findings which are referred to in this study are the ones obtained during excavations at Kashi-Rajghat (conducted under the supervision of A.K. Narain in the years 1957–1969), Kotwa, Aktha and Ramnagar (conducted by Vidula Jayaswal in the years 1994–2009).

AKITTA-JATAKA AND ARCHAEOLOGICAL REMAINS OF AKTHA

The description of the *Akitta-Jataka* reads as:

"Once upon a time, when Brahmadatta was king in Banaras, the Bodhisattva was born in the family of a Brahmin magnate, whose fortune accounted to eighty crores. They named him *Akitti,*... a sister was born and they gave her the name *Yasavati*. The Great Being proceeded at the age of sixteen years to Banaras, where he completed his education and then returned" (Cowell, E.B. 1990: 149).

The story further runs as, after death of his parents, at the age of sixteen he and his sister decided to become ascetic....

"So leaving the house with all its gold and precious metal, ... he and his sister departed. And the gate ... by which they went was Akitti Gate, and the landing stage they went down to the river, this also was called the Quay of Akitti" (Cowell, E.B.1990: 149).

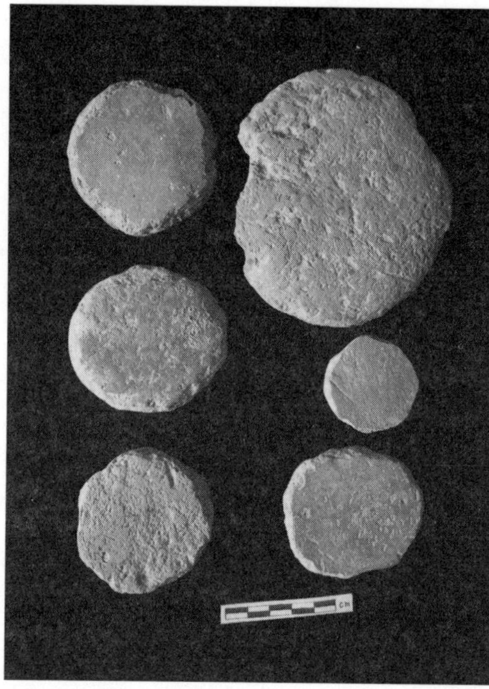

Fig. 6.3. *Kapala*, the earthen containers of Vedic Yajña from Maurya-Sunga periods, Aktha.

In the above-quoted passages, the following points are to be noted.

- That the Bodhisattva Akitti was born in a Brahmin family.
- That he went to receive education at Varanasi which was not the place where he resided.
- That a gate and the quay of the settlement where Bodhisattva Akitti was residing were named after him.

Comparable archaeological findings from Aktha are as below:

One of the most significant peripheral *muhallas* of modern Varanasi township, Aktha (83 01′ E and Lat. 25 22′ N) is situated near Paharia Mandi, which is the modern depot of fruits and vegetables. The ancient debris at this site was subject to archaeological probing in the years 2002 and 2004. Significance of this site was noted during the course of exploration carried out in this region in the year 1994 (Jayaswal, V. 1998:110-111), when a large conical mound locally known as *jhaua-jhadan* was visited. The morphological features of this mound indicated that a large stupa is buried beneath it. Early date of this structure could be

Fig. 6.4. View of Ramnagar mound with the Ramnagar fort on its one end.

assumed on account of the exposed mud bricks in the lower part of this stupa-mound. This mound is located on the confluence of the river Varuna and its tributary stream, Aktha/Narkhoh *nala*, at the southern periphery of Aktha.

The ancient settlement of Aktha is situated between two rivulets —the Narkhoh *nala* and the Aktha *nala*, which drain in to the river Varuna little south of the village. The site is very close to Sarnath, the Buddhist pilgrimage. Accumulation of a group of stone images at the raised ground close to Aktha village marked the centre of an ancient settlement. It is this place from where earlier an image of *Yaksha* was also discovered. Housed in the Saranath Museum, this image has been dated to around *c.* 1st/2nd century BCE (Lin-Bodien, C.G. 1981). Antiquity of Aktha was pushed back for about three to four centuries, by the discovery of Northern Black Polished Ware pot-sherds (dating between 6th and 4th centuries BCE), during exploration (Jayaswal, V. 1998:111). While excavations conducted at this site could establish that the earliest colonization of Varanasi region took

Fig. 6.5. Location of trenches at Oriyaghat, Ramnagar.

place here, on the left bank of Varuna which was on the main land route of Uttara Path. This was Aktha, near Sarnath. A continuous occupation from Later Vedic period (18th century BCE) to Late Kushana times (3rd century CE) has been exposed at Aktha (Jayaswal, V. 2009). Two assertions of Aktha findings are noteworthy for this case study. One, that this is the oldest known site of the region, which dates back to the Later Vedic times. The other, that it was a Brahmin settlement, where Vedic rituals were performed as daily routine, in all the identified historical periods.

The four comparable features of the narration of *Akitta-Jataka* mentioned earlier can be evaluated with the archaeological findings of Aktha, are as below.

1. Like other Jataka stories, tale of Bodhisattva Akitti too is of previous birth of Buddha, indicating remote antiquity of the event. The earliest occupation of Aktha is very early in date. The living floors of Period I of Aktha were full of burnt patches. The C-14 dates of charcoal samples obtained from these, date this horizon between 1700 and

Fig. 6.6. View of a habitation floor of Maurya period at Oriyaghat, Ramnagar.

1400 BCE. Incidentally, the early dates from this site are about nine hundred years older than the previously dated earliest habitation layers of Varanasi-Sarnath region. For, the earliest archaeological remains identified at Sarnath are of 3rd century BCE, while at Kashi-Rajghat (ancient city of Varanasi) it is of *c.* 800 BCE.

Though, Later Vedic Period falls beyond the suggested date boundary for the compilation of Jataka stories, it does establish great antiquity of human occupation in this region. To the compliers of the Jatakas, like *Akitta-Jataka* settlement of Aktha would be a suitable backdrop, for projecting authenticity of the theme picturing event of remote past.

2. In the first assertion mentioned above, the story mentions that Akitti was born in a Brahmin family. The archaeological contexts do suggest that Aktha was predominantly a Brahmin settlement. The habitation floors of all the four periods of Aktha—Later Vedic, Janapada, Maurya-Sunga and Kushana, retained traces of fire ritual

performances (Figs. 6.1 and 6.2). Association of ritual earthen pots with these floors were also recorded (Jayaswal, V. 2009). Pottery-discs, the *kapalas*, which have been identified as object used in Vedic rituals (Jayaswal, V. and M. Sharma. 2006), too fare well in all the periods (Fig. 6.3). On account of all these findings, Brahmin nature of the settlement is a logical deduction. The profound ritual activities at this site were found in association with deposits of 1st century BCE to 3rd century CE (Jayaswal, V. 2009).

Fig. 6.7. View of exposed part of the embankment of Maurya period, Oriyaghat, Ramnagar.

3. In the second assertion it was noted above that the Bodhisattva Akitti went to receive education at Varanasi which was a separate place than his residence. On account of archaeological investigations it can logically be held that settlement of Aktha was entirely separate from Kashi-Rajghat. The latter became the nucleus of Varanasi city, in Janapada and post-Janapada times. The history of growth of settlements in Varanasi region testifies that in the first stage only Aktha was occupied. While in Janapada times (about 800 BCE), the confluence of the rivers Ganga and Varuna, Kashi-Rajghat region was also inhabited. Aktha survived contemporary to Kashi-Rajghat till Late Kushana times. Thus, these two—Aktha and Kashi-Rajghat—were separate settlements between Janapada and Late Kushan times (*c.* 800 BCE–3rd century CE).

   - Bodhisattva Akitti, in the narration of *Akitta-Jataka*, appears to go to Kashi-Rajghat (ancient identified city of Varanasi) to receive education, from his native settlement Aktha.

Fig. 6.8. *Deluxe* and inscribed pottery of Maurya period from Oriyaghat, Ramnagar.

- It may further be concluded that the incidence of *Akitta-Jataka* was of post-Later Vedic period, since at Later Vedic times only one settlement, Aktha, was in existence. This would also mean that the composition of this story is post-Later Vedic.

4. A gate and the quay were named Akitti, after the name of Bodhisattva Akitti. The name Aktha of the modern village, where the ancient site is located sounds very alien to this region. The name of the rivulet Aktha *nala* is also unique. For, to assign one name to a settlement and also to a water channel is not a common practice in this part of the country. It is mentioned in the Jataka that due to the Bodhisattva, the Gate to Varanasi and the Quay, for going down the river, were named Akitti. Is it not possible that the name of the settlement and also the rivulet of the modern times is remembrance of one such old event, which gets focused in *Akitta-Jataka*?

The above elaborations suggest a number of comparable aspects between the narration of the *Akitta-Jataka* and the archaeological findings of Aktha. Although the above-discussed factors are not sufficient to testify the authenticity of the story under consideration, yet a hypothesis can be put forward for further investigation.

It can logically be held that mythological stories like Jataka were being woven within the culture environments of some ancient settlements, which had great antiquity and also were places of religious repute. Whether the events actually happened or were imagined may be difficult to ascertain. It may also be mentioned that, in case of *Akitta-Jataka*, the canvas on which the story was elaborated was the ancient settlement of

Fig. 6.9. General view of excavation of a sculptor village, Kotwa.

Aktha. Not only its remote antiquity and nature, predominately a Brahmin settlement, inspired the story, but the strong influence of Buddhism in this region too was a contributory factor. The close vicinity of Saranath, where Buddha had preached his first sermon, over the centuries, was centre for attraction for many—the monks, devotees of various sections of the society, including non-Buddhists. Conversion to Buddhism too must have been a regular practice here. Stories of conversion of Brahmins and others must be in circulation. The process of convergence also appears to be responsible for the formulation of some of the mythological stories of the Jatakas.

KACHHAPA-JATAKA AND THE ARCHAEOLOGICAL REMAINS OF RAMNAGAR

The following portion of the narration of *Kacchapa-Jataka* (No. 178) is noteworthy for our case study.

"Once upon a time when Brahmadatta was reigning in Banaras, the Bodhisatva was born in a village as a potter's son. He plied the potter's trade."

Fig. 6.10. Exposed chiselling floors of Kushan period, Kotwa.

"At that time there lay a great natural lake close by the great river of Banaras. When there was much water, river and lake were one; but when the water was low, ... they were apart."

"Now fish and tortoises know by instinct when the year will be rainy and when there will be a drought. So at the time of our story the fish and tortoise which lived in that lake knew there would be a drought; and when the two were one water, they swam out of the lake into the river. But, there was one tortoise that would not go into the river, because, said he, 'here I was born, and here I have grown up, and here is my parents' home: leave it I cannot.'"

"Then in the hot season the water all dried up. He dug a hole and buried himself, just in the place where the Bodhisatva was used to come for the clay. There the Bodhisatva came for some clay; with a big spade he dug down, till he cracked the tortoise's shell, turning him out on the ground". ...(Cowell, E.B. 1990).

Noteworthy points in the above-quoted passages are the following.

- That there was a large natural pond near the mighty river Ganga in Varanasi.
- That the Bodhisattva was born in a potter's family.
- That for the earthen pots, clay was obtained from the dried bed of ponds.
- That there were traders who indulged in the trading of earthen pots.

Comparable instances come from the ancient settlement on the left bank of the river Ganga at Ramnagar.

Situated on the right bank of the river Ganga, Ramnagar (83° 17′ E and 25° 16′ N) is a small settlement known for the fort of Maharaja of Banaras.

Ancient habitation of Ramnagar has a wide spread—a stretch of about 3 kilometres between the Fort (located on the northern end of the mound)—and the Shastri Bridge (on the National Highway). But, the ancient settlement appears to be confined to the bank and does not extend beyond half a kilometre from the riverside. The riverside near Ramnagar has high embankment (about 15 metres high from the water level), over which rests ancient deposits (of about 10-15 metres). The most promising topography of the ancient site is deep erosion and gullies, which appear to dissect the bank in a series of small units or mounds. The promising heights are utilised as Ghats. Each Ghat, be it Hanumanghat, Kuttaghat, Golaghat, Koriyaghat, Pipraghat or Oriyaghat, is on one mound and is used by local people as bathing place and/or navigation port. That is because the depth of water at these places is considerable.

During archaeological investigations conducted at Oriyaghat, Ramnagar, it could be ascertained that this region was under occupation between Maha-Janapada and Late Kushana periods. The location of this site and the cultural remains exposed give clear indication that this was a trade-based settlement. For, being located on the bank of the river Ganga, it was well connected with various parts of the Ganga Plains on one hand and on the other it was also by the side of the main land route, connecting the Middle Ganga Plains with the Deccan.

The archaeological horizons significant for this case study were:

1. Location of a pond by the side of the river Ganga, at Oriyaghat, has direct relevance to this case study. The main trench which was dug up to the depth of 10 metres was noteworthy. The earliest cultural layer (the lowest layer 16) was overlying a dried pond bed deposit (Jayaswal, V. and M. Kumar 2006). The sampling and testing of sediments of the natural soil revealed that over a dried bed of a pond, rested an Aeolian deposit of soil blown from the Vindhyas. This indicated that there was a long time gap between the drying of the pond and occupation of its bed for habitation purposes.

   Incidentally the earliest archaeological horizon at this site, which comes from one metre thick deposit (layer 16) is dateable from *c.* 14th century to 13th century BCE. Implying that the existence of the pond and its drying up were older events than the above time bracket. How old was this event, is the question which needs to be addressed. A complete sequence of sediments of the Ramnagar bank could be prepared (Jayaswal V. and M. Kumar 2006 and Shukla, U.K. and N.J. Raju 2008). Shukla also has investigated other parts of Varanasi and has studied the deposits of Varanasi with a view to reconstructing the history of the water channels in general and the river Ganga in particular. Evidences for tectonic movements have been recorded in the region, which happened in around 7000 BP (Srivastava, P. and U.K. Shukla 2009). As a result of which, the banks of the river Ganga were uplifted and acquired the present form. Details of this study have been incorporated in this volume. It may be held that not only river channel was trapped between the left and right banks, but also ponds located on the banks drained out. The deep gullies and dissects of the bank at Ramnagar are reminiscent of this event. Thus, draining/drying of the pond at Oriyaghat may also be accepted to be part of this geological event, which took place thousands of years before the place was colonised. The pond, abode of the Kachchapa of the *Kachchapa-Jataka* too, according to the concept of the Jataka, was a very old incidence.

2. The second assertion that with good rains the water level of the river used to rise up to the level of the pond, is indirectly supported by the archaeological findings at Oriyaghat as a massive platform/ embankment was exposed at this locality (Fig. 6.7).

   The pond mentioned in the *Kachhapa-Jataka*, resembles the one, traces of which were obtained in the archaeological digs. In the periphery of the mound (Trench C′ 3) a very imposing platform made of rammed brick bats, potsherds and *kankar* was encountered at the depth of 4.30 m. This 0.78 m thick structure was superimposed by eleven layers, assigned to Late NBPW, Kushana and Gupta periods. Below the platform lay five distinct layers (12-16), which yielded very good quality of NBPW potsherds in large quantities. Occurrence of good quality of NBPW sherds in the layers 13, 14 and 15, suggests that the platform was constructed sometime during the Late Northern Black Polished Ware period.

   This platform (Fig. 6.7) served as protective device from the rising water from the river Ganga. Evidence for flood was also unearthed from the adjoining area (Trenches C′3 and B′2-C′2 at the depth of about 5 metres below the surface). Similar evidence was also unearthed from the deposits of Period IB, at Kashi-Rajghat, which has been interpreted as, "...it was a clay embankment which served to prevent the scouring of the banks and also to stop the flood water entering the habitational area" (Narain, A.K. and T.N. Roy. 1976: 23). The settlement of Ramnagar, as was the case with capital Varanasi, was experiencing frequent floods when the water level was reaching the spot where pond had existed, a situation narrated in the Jataka.

Incidentally, the topography of Kashi-Rajghat mound is similar to Oriyaghat, Ramnagar, as both are located on the cutting side of the river and over a thick alluvial deposit. Traces of pond at Kashi-Rajghat have not been recorded, while its existence is attested at Oriyaghat, Ramnagar. It may be held that at the time of settlement, the pond had dried up completely. But the old situation in which water of the river and pond could be one, possibly remained in the memory and the folk tales.

3. It has been mentioned in *Kachchapa-Jataka* that the Bodhisattva was born as a son of a potter, and was indulging in the trade of pottery. Oriyaghat was a pottery-producing settlement is an archaeological deduction, which is relevant to the present theme.

Digging of the peripheral area (Trench C'2) exposed pottery-making spot. Not only NBPW potsherds were found in very large numbers here, but these evinced a range of colours resulting from various types of firing conditions. Also thick layers of whitish ash bands were found in succession in which some half-baked potsherds were also embedded. This locality, thus, was identified as the production center of the *deluxe* ware, the Northern Black Polished ware. It is logical to visualise that these worshops were owned by pottery traders. There are quite a few indications that *deluxe* ware like the NBPW was traded.

Besides, inscribed potsherds from Ramnagar were recovered from the Early and Late Northern Black Polished Ware horizons (Fig. 6.8). Though NBPW and Black Slipped Ware potsherds have also been reported from Period IC and IB of Kashi-Rajghat, which have been classified under potsherds with graffiti marks (Narain, A.K. and T.N. Roy 1977: 115-116; Pl. XXVII), in numerical count and variety these are restricted. This is particularly noteworthy, since the area excavated at Rajghat was considerably larger than the restricted digging at Ramnagar. That the

NBPW produced at Ramnagar was item of export is also attested by the negligible number of shards of the ceramic found from the contemporary habitation layer of Oriyaghat (Trench A1). On the other hand, the capital city of Kashi Janapada, Kashi-Rajghat was using this ceramic in large quantities, many of which were also inscribed (Narain, A.K. and T.N. Roy 1976). The evidence thus is that the NBPW workshops of Ramnagar, were owned by traders, who were marking their goods before exporting to other settlements.

The above account reveals a number of similarities between the description of *Kachchapa-Jataka* and the archaeological and geological findings of Ramnagar. Whether the theme of *Kachchapa-Jataka* was solely based on this settlement or it represents a historical, geo-physical and socio-cultural make-up of early historical period is a matter of debate.

VARANASI SETTLEMENT OF JATAKA-STORIES

A list of names is available for Varanasi in the Jatakas. In *Yuvanjaya-Jataka* (No. 460) the description runs as, "Once upon a time, a king named Sabhadatta reigned in the city of Ramma. The place which we now call Banaras" (Cowell, E.B. 1990: 75). Ramma city here is mentioned as one of the localities of Varanasi. The others being Sudassana city in the Cullasutasoma birth (Jataka No. 525), Surundhana of Udaya birth (Jataka No. 458), Brahmavadhana in Sonandana birth (Jataka No. 532), and Pupphavati in the Khandahala birth (120). "In this manner its name changes on each occasion" (Cowell, E.B. 1990: 75-76). The list of names mentioned in the Jataka stories for ancient Varanasi raises such questions as, whether these were different names for one settlement, ancient Varanasi? Or, there were different settlements/localities within the boundaries of ancient Varanasi? At present, it may be difficult to side with one or the other possibility in affirmative. But, to me it appears that the list mentioned above refers to various localities of Varanasi city. For, the archaeological remains suggest that the settlement of Varanasi had shifted from one to the other place during its long history. Similar view was also expressed by Sherring as early as 1868 (Sherring, M.A. 1990: 33-34), who writes, "There is still a scattered population on the southern bank of the Barna", and "to the north of the present city, between it and the Barna". "The tendency of Banaras to change its boundaries, for it shifts continually in a southwesterly direction, is well illustrated by the position of the three fortresses—Rajghat, Sivalayaghat and Ramnagar"

(Sherring, M.A. 1990: 33-34). The distribution and antiquity of archaeological sites in Varanasi region correspond with the hypothesis of shifting of settlement from north to south-east and towards west and south-west along the river Ganges. Sherring's hypothesis is partly supported, but needs some modification.

Excavations at Aktha reveal that perhaps the earliest part of ancient Varanasi was located on the confluence of Aktha and Narkhoh *nalas* and Varuna river. It was inhabited around 18th century BCE. It was only after about nine centuries that Kashi-Rajghat was selected as dwelling area. Aktha and Kashi-Rajghat appear to survive as parallel and twin settlements for next five centuries. It was around *c*. 4th century BCE that Kashi-Rajghat entered the stage of urbanization, while Aktha with its rural base receded to the status of peripheral settlement/locality till its last days (*c*. 3rd century CE). It was in the second stage that confluence of Varuna with Ganga River was occupied. On account of excavations at Kashi-Rajghat, remains of ancient city of Varanasi were identified in this locality. This has been identified as the 'first fortress' by Sherring. The earliest habitation of this locality was dated to *c*. 800 BCE. But, the urban format of Varanasi, as is evidenced by excavations, came to existence around 3rd/4th century BCE. (Narain, A.K. and T.N. Roy. 1976: 22). Kashi-Rajghat appears to lost its glory some time during Gupta period. Thus, in the third stage the territorial expansion of the city was towards Pucca Mahal area (west of Kashi-Rajghat) which still is the heart of Varanasi city. This tendency is well recorded in the accounts of the Chinese traveller Weing Chuang, who visited Varanasi in the 7th century CE. The nucleus of the city as per his description was located south-west of Sarnath (Watters, T. 1988), which has been calculated by this author to be the Pucca Mahal area (Jayaswal, V. 2011, 2012). Still later, the boundaries of this city extended up to the Assi River. On account of these findings successive expansion appears to be the most prominent pattern, for the historical make-up of Varanasi. Sherring's second fortress, the Sivalayaghat also fits well with the other remains indicating expansion of the city towards Assi. But, Ramnagar fort is a much later construction. Beneath it lies thick debris of ancient settlement which was contemporary to Kashi-Rajghat.

It can further be ascertained that the nucleus of the settlement was also surrounded by dense concentrations of supporting settlements (Jayaswal, V. 1998: 119-211). These were feeding centres of the city and dwelling areas of the craftsmen. It has been shown from the excavations of the sites like Kotwa and Asapur, for instance, that these rural-based locales were sculpture-making centres or dwelling-cum-workshop sites (Jayaswal, V.1998). Exposure of a number of chiselling floors at Kotwa is particularly noteworthy (Fig. 6.9). This sculptor village was in existence from Kushana (Fig. 6.10) to medieval times. Some of these craft villages too form theme of Jatakas, like *Babbu-Jataka* (No. 137), which describes "Bodhisattva born in the family of a stonecutter, and growing up became expert in working stones". Further, it is mentioned as part of the narration that, "At the time of our story the Bodhisattva was quarrying and shaping stones on the site of this deserted village" (Cowell, E.B. 1990: 295). It appears that the narration of *Babbu-Jataka* is a mirror of the contemporary times, which on account of the archaeological findings at Kotwa may be assigned a date bracket of *c.* beginning of the Common Era to 10th/11th centuries, when stone-cutting in Varanasi was practised as one of the most prominent indigenous crafts.

DISCUSSION

As shown above, the point of similarities between the narration of the Jatakas and the archaeological findings of Varanasi are many. But, the question is about their authenticity for historical reconstruction. Whether the events and scenes occurring in the Jatakas were factual and had happened in the past, or were imagination based on general occurrences, are difficult to comprehend. For instance, on account of the close similarities between the make-up of the ancient settlement Aktha and the mythological story of *Akitta-Jataka*, though both appear to be interlinked, yet it may not be logical to accept without question mark, that Aktha was the adopted backdrop or the place where the events of *Akitta-Jataka* took place. Likewise, identification of Ramanagar, as the place of happenings of *Kachchapa-Jataka*, though may be suggestive, is not beyond debate. The shifting settlement pattern of ancient Varanasi, which appears to be reflected in the Jatakas, in terms of different names for Varanasi, too is interesting. Similar pattern may be noticed in the settlement history of Varanasi region, which comes to light on account of the archaeological studies. But, in this case also one is handicapped. Because, the question of identification of individual names listed in the Jatakas remains unsloved. One wonders if some methodology cannot be developed which can help in drawing logical and meaningful inferences from culturally rich compilations like the Jatakas?

Dating of Jataka stories with the help of scientific studies is another desirable line to be attempted. Study of the select Jatakas and the comparable archaeo-geological data does suggest probability to assign a time bracket to these compositions. For instance, the date for the *Akitta-Jataka* could be between 3rd–2nd century BCE and 1st–2nd century CE, when both Aktha and Kashi-Rajghat enjoyed separate and significant status. Similarly, the time bracket of *Kachchapa-Jataka* could be around 4th–3rd century BCE, as this was the time of the production and trading of *deluxe* ware NBPW in large scale in the Varanasi region. But, these dates too remain tentative in the absence of availability of foolproof scientific methods.

REFERENCES

Cowell, E.B. (ed.), 1990, *The Jataka or the Stories of Buddha's Former Births,* Vols. II-V, (Reprinted), Munshiram Manoharlal, Delhi.

Jayaswal, V., 1998, *From Stone Quarry to Sculpturing Workshop: A Report on the Archaeological Investigations around Chunar, Varanasi and Sarnath,* Agam Kala Prakashan, Delhi.

Jayaswal, V., 2002, 'Aktha: A Satellite Settlement of Sarnath, Varanasi (Report of Excavations Conducted in the Year 2002)', *Bharati,* Bulletin of the Department of Ancient Indian History, Culture and Archaeology, BHU 26: 61-180.

Jayaswal, V., 2009, *Ancient Varanasi: An Archaeological Perspective,* Aryan Books International, New Delhi.

Jayaswal, V., 2011, *Adi Kashi se Varanasi tak* (Hindi), Aryan Books International, New Delhi.

Jayaswal, V., 2012, 'The Ganga in Varanasi: Myth and History', *Jnana-Pravah: Fifteen Glorious Years.* [J. Chatterjee (ed.)], Jnana-Pravaha, South of Samne Ghat, Varanasi, pp. 95-101.

Jayaswal, V. and Manoj Kumar, 2006, 'Excavations at Ramnagar, 2005-6: Discovery of Supporting Settlement of Ancient Varanasi', *Puratattva* 36: 85-92.

Jayaswal, V. and Meera Sharma, 2006, 'Pottery Disc: The Kapala of Vedic Yajna', *Purabharati: Studies in Early Historical Archaoelogy and Buddhism* (Commemoration Volume in Respect of Prof. B.P. Sinha), B.R. Mani and S.C. Saran (eds.), Sharda Publishing House, Delhi, pp. 38-47.

Lin-Bodien, C.G., 1981, 'An Early Yaksha from Aktha near Sarnath (Varanasi Dist. U.P.)', *Chhavi: Rai Krishnadas Felicitation,* Vol. 2, Bharat Kala Bhavan, BHU, Varanasi.

Narain, A.K. and T.N. Roy, 1976, *Excavations at Rajghat (1957-58; 1960-65): The Cuttings, Stratification and Structures*, Part I, Department of Ancient Indian History, Culture and Archaeology, Banaras Hindu University, Varanasi.

Narain, A.K. and T.N. Roy, 1977, *Excavations at Rajghat (1957-58; 1960-65): The Pottery*, Part II, Department of Ancient Indian History, Culture and Archaeology, Banaras Hindu University, Varanasi.

Narain, A.K. and P. Singh, 1977, *Excavations at Rajghat (1957-58; 1960-65): Small Finds*, Part III, Department of Anceint Indian History, Culture and Archaeology, Banaras Hindu University, Varanasi.

Sherring, M.A., 1990 (Reprinted), *Benares: The Sacred City of the Hindus in Ancient and Modern times* (First printed in 1868), Low Price Publications, Delhi.

Srivastava, P. and U.K. Shukla, 2009, 'Quaternary Evolution of the Ganga River System: New Quartz Ages and a Review of Luminescence Chronology', *Himalayan Geology* 30: 85-94.

Shukla, U.K. and N.J. Raju, 2008, 'Migration of the Ganga River and Its Implications on Hydro-Geological Potential of Varanasi Area', *Journal of Earth System Science* 117: 489-498, U.P., India.

Watters, Thomas, 1988, *On Yuan Chwang's Travels in India 629-647* AD, Vol. II, (Reprinted, First published in 1905), Asian Educational Services, New Delhi.

7

Myths Related to Avimuktakshetra

Prachi Virag Sontakke

INTRODUCTION

Kashi, the city luminous, is known by various names. Puranas refer to it as *Avimukta, Anandakanana, Mahasmashana, Rudravas, Anandarupa, Shankarpuri, Shivapuri, Dharamakshetra*, Varanasi, etc. (Chandramouli, 1995:6). Each of these names has a special meaning, so as to reflect one or other historic-mythological event related to Kashi. *Avimukta* is no exception. It denotes one of the *kshetra*s of Kashi and has its own history. The focus of the present paper is to scrutinise some select, but prominent myths related to *Avimuktakshetra*, and identify through these the possible happenings of climatic, geomorphic and ancient human endeavours in Kashi.

The main source for studying the myths of *Avimuktakshetra* is Kashikhanda of *Skanda Purana*. *Skanda Purana* is named after Skanda, son of Lord Shiva and the commander of the celestial armies, who is said to have related it and proclaimed Saivite doctrines in it. Texts which form part of *Skanda Purana* mention six Samhitas, namely *Sanatkumariya, Suta, Brahmi, Vaishnavi, Sankari* and *Sauri-Samhita* (Winternitz, 1987:545). Kashikhanda is a part of *Sankari Samhita* and it deals with the Shiva temples in the neighbourhood of Kashi, along with the sanctity of the city. At places, *Linga, Vamana* and *Padama Purana* are also made use of.

It may be mentioned at the very outset that the proposed attempt is challenging, for two reasons, 'one, because of the nature of the source', and the other, due to the lack of reliable chronology of the ancient texts, which record the myths.

Formulation of a myth, mostly, is an admixture of a factual happening and imagination biased by religious faith. As the time passes, the original myth, closer to the actual happening, drifts towards religious belief and connotations. Thus, the form of myth which reaches us today, after a long time, is generally overpowered by secondary accretions. As is suggested by MacDonell, it may therefore be hard to ascertain the original form of the events or episodes in the myths (MacDonell, 1974:1).

The problem of dating of the ancient texts has always been a matter of debate. This is because most Sanskrit works neither mention the date of their composition nor the place of compilation (Vaidya 1986:2). Nevertheless, scholars like Winternitz, Max Müller, Hazra, Vaidya and others have tried to ascertain their chronology on the basis of their contents. R.C. Hazra places *Skanda Purana* between 700–1400 CE (Hazra, 1987:165) while S.C.Banerjee keeps it in between 700 and 1050 CE (Banerjee, 1991: 12). The former also holds *Padma Purana* and *Linga Purana* as belonging to the date bracket of 950–1400 CE, and earlier than 1000 CE, respectively (Hazra, 1987:112, 95) while the latter believes them to be composed between 3rd and 4th centuary CE and 800 and 1000 CE, respectively (Banerjee, 1991: 12). *Vamana Purana* likewise falls between 700 and 1000 CE time frame (Hazra, 1987:80). It is significant here to note that these dates refer to the date of composition of works but the events which are described in these compositions refer to remote past.

In spite of the aforesaid limitations, study of myths is an imperative exercise, as these form an integral part of our culture. The need for scientific evaluation of myths, thus is a much awaited necessity, which should be undertaken in a big way.

THE MYTH ON KSHETRAS

Concept of *kshetras* relating to Kashi is very well documented in the Puranas. Terms like *Varanasikshetra* (*Vamana Purana*.3.29), *Avimuktakshetra* (Kashikhanda 26.31) and *Anandavanakshetra* (Kashikhanda 39.74) are used explicitly in context of Kashi. Often these *kshetra*s are used as synonyms in Pauranic verses. But this was not so as these *kshetra*s did not denote the same location. It appears that they represented different localities distributed within a geographical unit (Kashi) across time. Therefore a chronological order of development may also have existed in relation to these *kshetras*. This is traced with the help of references from Kashikhanda.

Kashikhanda 26.24-27 tells us that *Avimuktakshetra* was created by Lord Shiva. Same idea is reverberated in Kashikhanda 26.28 and 26.31 thus

न यदा भूमिवलयं न यदाऽपां समुद्र भवः।
तदा विहर्तुमीशेन क्षेत्रमेत द्विनिर्मितम्।।
का॰ ख॰ 26. 28

(i.e. when there was no land, nor water was created, at that time, this *kshetra* was created for roaming of lord).

अविमुक्तं तदाश्भ्य क्षेत्रमेतदुदीर्यते।
पर्यंकभूते शिवयोर्निरन्तरसुखास्पदम्।।
का॰ ख॰ 26. 31

(i.e. from then onwards this *kshetra* was called as *Avimuktakshetra*. This is the comfortable bed of Shivashiva)

This indicates that from the time this *kshetra* was created by Lord Shiva, it was known as *Avimukta*. But Kashikhanda 26.36 brings forth another for this very region.

ज्ञेयानि सर्वालिंगानि तास्मिन्नानन्दकानने।
अविमुक्मभितिख्यातमासीदित्थंघटो्द्भव।।
का॰ ख॰ 26. 36

(i.e. thus, this region became famous as *Avimukta* and *Anandakanana).*

This way, *Avimukta* and *Anandavana* are identified as belonging to one location. But the question is of the two which one is earlier? If we go by Kashikhanda (26.24 and 26.27), *Avimukta* seems to be an earlier establishment. However, another verse of Kashikhanda 39.74 tells us that *Avimukta* was known as *Anandavana* in earlier times.

पुरानन्दवन नाम क्षेत्रमेतत् प्रकीर्तितम्।
अविमुक्तं तदारभ्य नामाऽस्य प्रथितं भुवि।।
का॰ ख॰ 39. 74

(i.e. name of this *kshetra* in earlier times was *Anandavana* but since then its name *Avimukta* became popular in world).

Kashikhanda 26.34 also reflects the same thought.

अस्यानन्दहेतुत्वाद विमुक्तमनन्तरम्।
आनन्दकन्द बीजानामङ्कुराणि यतस्ततः।।
का० ख० 26. 34

(i.e. this *kshetra* is the cause of pleasure. That is why, in earlier times, Pinaki had named it *Anandavana*. Later it was known as *Avimukta*).

Following these two verses, it appears that *Anandavana* was in existence before it was identified as *Avimukta*. This way, *Anandavana* seems earlier than *Avimukta*. Thus, Kashikhanda gives two opposite ideas with regard to the chronology of *Anandavana* and *Avimukta*. But it appears that both *Anandavana* and *Avimukta* were a part of the same geographical unit constituting two settlements. With time, some new settlements also came up in the same geographical setting. This would mean the expansion and exploitation of the concerned region on a greater scale. It will also indicate that the ecology of this geographical setting was conducive for the rise of new settlements. This is also verified by literature where *Anandavana* and *Avimukta* are identified with new locales of habitation. We find in Kashikhnada 32.112-113 that *Anandavana* is identified with Varanasi.

अत्रानन्दवने देवि भृतानां मदनुग्रहात्।
वपुस्त्व भष्ततां प्राप्तमपुनाभविनस्तुते।।
भविनो ये विथद्यन्ते वाराणस्या ममाज्ञाया।
तेषां बीजानि दग्धानि रमशानज्वलदाग्निना।।
का० ख० 32. 112–113

(i.e. whosoever dies in this *Anandavana* attains *amrit pada* by my grace and they are not born again. If who so ever is born, dies in Varanasi, their seeds of *karma* are burned in the funeral fire by my order).

The same is true for *Avimukta* too. The area between Asi and Varuna is also called *Avimuktakshetra*. Third chapter of *Vamana Purana* and Kashikhanda 5.25 states that the region between Asi and Varunas is *Avimukta* (Sherring, 1990: xvii-xix).

वरणापिंगलानाडी तदन्तस्त्वविमुक्तकम्।।
सा सुषुम्नापरानाडी त्रयं वाराणसी त्वसौ
का० ख० 5. 25–26

(i.e. O Arune ! world famous Jabali sage has said that Asi and Varana rivers are *ida nadi* and *pingala nadi*. Between these two is that

Avimuktakshetra Kashi. This Kashi is *sushumna nadi*. Varanasi comprises of these three *nadis*).

Interestingly, in the same verse, uniformity of *Avimukta* with Kashi and Varanasi is also suggested.
Region between Asi and Varana is also called as Varanasi in *Vamana Purana*.

चरणाद् दक्षिणात्तत्स्य विनिर्याता सरिद्वश
विश्रुते वरणेत्येव सर्वपापहरा शुभा
सव्यादन्या द्वितीया च असिरित्येव विश्रुता
ताभ्यां मध्ये तु यो दे शस्त्रत्क्षेत्रं योगशायिनः
त्रॅलोक्य प्रवर तीर्थ सर्वपापप्रमोचनम्
न ताहशोऽस्ति गगने न भूम्यां न रसातले।
तत्रास्ति नगरी पुण्या ख्याता वाराणसी शुभा।।
वामनपुराण 3.27.30

(i.e from the southern foot came well-talked, pious, sin-freeing Varana river and from the left foot came the famous Asi river. The region between them is the region of Yoga. It is the best in three worlds and this *tirtha* frees one from all sins. There is nothing like it in sky, earth or *rasatala*. Pious and famous Varanasi city is there).

This nature of growth of settlements in a distinct geographical unit is also proved archaeologically. Various locales of human habitation like Aktha, Rajghat, Ramnagar, Pucca Mahal area, etc. were identified to be present at different time frames within Kashi (Jayaswal, 2009: 213). Thus, what we call *Avimukta* is one of the old establishments of Kashi. This way, the myths relating to *Avimuktakshetra* will have their bearing on the history of Kashi.

MYTHS ON DRAUGHT CONDITIONS

Kashikhanda (39.26-42) describes existence of a very dry spell in Kashi region.

पादमे कल्पे पुरावृत्ते मनोः स्वायम्भुवेऽन्तरे।
अनावृष्टिरभूद्विप्र सर्वभूतप्रकम्पिनी।। 26
तया तु षष्टिहायिन्या पीड़िताः प्राणिनोऽखिलाः।
केचिदम्बुधितीरषु गिरिद्रोणीशु केचन।। 27
महानिम्नेषु कच्छेपुमुनिवृत्त्या जनाः स्थिताः।
अरण्यान्यवनिर्जाता ग्रामखर्वटवर्जिता।। 28
का॰ ख॰ 39. 26–28

(i.e. in the Swayambhuva Manvantara of the last Padamkalpa, there was no rain for 60 years everywhere. Due to this, all living beings were troubled. During that period, people started moving towards mountain caves, seashores and to the lower areas with water and lived a life of asceticism. Whole earth was devoid of cities and villages and became a forest.)

Seeing such a messy state of things, Brahma was troubled and requested Ripunjaya, who was penancing in *Avimukta*, to take over as king and henceforth be known as Divodasa. Then Divodasa asked Brahma "Are there not other kings on this earth? Why do you say so to me?" to which Brahma replied:

त्वयि राज्यं प्रकुर्वाणे देवो वृष्टि विधास्यति।
पापनिष्ठे च वै राज्ञि न देवो वर्षते पुनः।।
का॰ ख॰ 39. 42

(i.e. "Rajan, when you will reign, it will rain. If the king is evil, then it will never rain".)

Kashikhanda (39.44-46) tells us that Divodasa agrees but put forwards a condition that he will rule only when all gods will leave earth and will move to heaven. Brahma informs Shiva of the rainless 60 years and appointment of Divodasa as the solution and also his condition before taking over as the king (Kashikhanda 39.61-64). As a solution, Shiva accepted the invitation by Madar and moved to Madaranchal but remained present in Kashi in the form of *linga*.

मन्दराद्रि गतेनापि क्षेत्रं नैतात्पिनाकिना।
विमुक्तं लिगरूपेण अविमुक्तमतः स्मृतम्।।
पुरा नन्दवनं नाम श्रेतमेतत् प्रकीर्तितम्।
अविमुक्तं तदारभ्य नामाऽस्य प्रथितं भुवि।।
का॰ ख॰ 39. 73.74

(i.e. even after going to Mandaranchal, Pinakapani did not leave this *kshetra*. This *kshetra* was *Anandavana* before but since then it became popular in the world as *Avimukta*)

The above-mentioned narrations point towards the following:

- There was a dry spell in *Anandavana* in last Padmakalpa which lasted for 60 years and resulted in severe drought conditions. Since one is not very sure about the date of Padamakalpa, one wonders if it is possible to scientifically identify this time frame by conducting geological and geomorphic investigations?

- The problem was so acute that people started migrating to regions with water which indicates that drought was restricted to *Anandavana* region only. There were other areas which had water, attracting immigrants. Is it not an indication that the said drought was a micro-climatic phenomena, confined to Varanasi region? If so, is it possible to ascertain this assumption by scientific studies?
- One also wonders if migration of people from *Avimukta* to other areas, can be shown through scientific data? If so, the event mentioned in the myth can also be given a tentative time bracket. It may be recalled, that at the archaeological sites in the Kashi region one finds evidence for desertion in the post-Kushana times, and the next inhabitant of the Gupta and post-Gupta times select new locales for dwelling (Jayaswal, V. 2009). Though historically this event appears quite late (2nd/3rd century CE), but, for the compiler of the text of Kashikhanda (medieval times), would this incident not be of remote past?

MYTHS ON KUNDAS OF KASHI

Various parts of Kashikhanda (33.3-26) describe nature and history of *kundas* (the tanks), one of the unique features of Varanasi settlement.

अनादिसिद्धे संसारे पुरा देवयुगे मुने
प्राप्तः कुतश्चिदीशानश्चरन् स्वैरमितस्ततः
न वर्शान्ति यदाऽभ्राणि न प्रावर्तन्त निम्नगाः
जलाभिलाशो न यदा स्नानपानादिकर्मणि
क्षारस्वादूदयोरेव यदासीज्जलदर्शनम
पृथिव्यां नर संचारे वर्तमान क्वाचित क्वाचित।
का॰ ख॰ 33. 35

(i.e. when there was Satyuga period, then clouds didn't rain on earth. Rivers also didn't flow. In that time, people didn't want water even in activities like bathing and drinking. Then water was visible only in the oceans and spread of humans started here and there on earth. At that time, a *dikpala* named Ishan roamed here and there and reached this place.)

अस्येशानस्य तल्लिंग दृश्ट्वेच्छेत्यभवन्तदा
स्नपयामि महाल्लिंग कलशैः शीतलेर्जलॅः
का॰ ख॰ 33. 16

(i.e. seeing that *linga, dikpala* Ishan wanted to bathe that very *mahalinga* with cold water of *kalasha*).

चरवान च त्रिशूलेन दक्षिणाशोपकण्ठतः।
कुण्डं प्रचण्डवेगेन रूद्रो रूद्रवपुर्धरः।।
पृथिव्यावरणाम्भांसि निष्क्रान्तानि तदा मुने।
भू प्रमाणाद्दशगुणैर्यैरियं वसुधावृता।।
का० ख० 33. 17—18

(i.e. then Rudramurti Ishan dug a *kunda* nearby, in the southern direction, by the might of his trident. Then from that *kunda*, water came out which was ten times the cover of earth and extent of land).

सहस्त्रधारेः कलशैः स ईशानो घटोद्भव।
सहस्त्रकृत्वः स्नपयामास संहृष्टमानसः।।
का० ख० 33. 26

(i.e. from that waters he happily bathed the *linga*, thousands of times with the water of thousands of perforated *kalashas*).

The following derivations are significant to note.

- There was a time in Satayuga period when water was a scarce commodity in Varanasi region, the *Anandavana* of the time.
- This drought appears to be the result of the lack of rains in the region.
- To meet the scarcity of water, large *kunda*s were dug in Varanasi. Mythology narrates digging of such *kundas* as the one at Jnana Vapi which was dug by Ishan.
- The *kundas* appear to be of three different types:
    - (a) Newly constructed *kunda*s, which were fresh dug-outs.
    - (b) Utilization of the source of water of the palaeochannels for *kunda*s.
    - (c) Parts of palaeochannels altered as *kunda*s.

A detailed geomorphologic plotting of palaeochannels of Varanasi region, and location of the tanks, would ascertain the nature as well as the factual data of the *kunda*s of this region.

DISCUSSION

The above-mentioned myths narrating *kundas* assume great significance when they are seen in the context of occurrence of so many *kundas, vapis* and *sarovaras* in Kashi (fig. 1). Kashikhanda refers to 88 *hrads* and 62 *kunda*s in Varanasi. Kashikhanda (43.63) tells us that in the reign of Divodasa, there were people at every step who abound in making wells, *vapis*, ponds and gardens. However when we see *kunda*-making tradition at other religious places, we find that this tradition is not as popular as it is in the region of study. Be it Prayag, Haridwar, Gaya, Nasik or Kanchi; *kunda*s were not much in use. Though in Ayodhya and Mathura, there are more *kunda*s than in the above-mentioned places but their numbers are very small when compared to the counts of *kunda*s in Kashi. This proliferation of *kunda*s in Kashi certainly appears to have deep-rooted cause in its history.

In the end, it could be said that though the scholars have generally preferred to discuss the nature and environment of the past with the help of scientific studies, however, hidden in the obscure spirals of the myths and legends of early Indian literature are the memories of ancient environmental and natural forces as experienced by man. These may not be the most potent rememberances but they do embody man's early explanations of the world he lived in, his environment and the forces governing his life. Moreover, during the last few decades, hydrographers, geographers and geologists have applied their specialised knowledge to the study of geophysical systems in India. Archaeological data relevant to it has also been discovered. Time, therefore, seems ripe to reopen a discussion which will elucidate the relationship of the accounts in our literature with reality of situation. Thus, archaeological evidence, when applied to narrative accounts and scientific data, is bound to expand our vistas of knowledge about the past environments in particular and contribution of myths to Indian culture in general.

REFERENCES

Banerjee, S.C., 1991, *Studies in the Mahapuranas,* Punthi Pustak, Calcutta.

Chandramouli, K., 1995, *Kashi—The City Luminous,* Rupa and Co., New Delhi.

Jayaswal, Vidula, 2009, *Ancient Varanasi: An Archaeological Perspective (Excavations at Aktha),* Aryan Books International, New Delhi.

Hazra, R.C., 1987 (reprint), *Studies in the Puranic Records on Hindu Rites and Customs,* Motilal Banarasidass, Varanasi. First published in 1940, Dacca.

Macdonell, A.A., 1974 (reprint), *Vedic Mythology,* Motilal Banarasidass, Varanasi. First published in 1898, Strassburg.

Motichandra, 1985 (2nd edition), *Kashi ka Itihasa: Vaidic Kala se Arvachina Yug tak ka Rajnaitika-Samskritika Sarvekshana,* Vishwavidyalaya Prakashana, Varanasi. First published in 1962.

Sherring, M.A., 1990 (reprint), *Benares: The Sacred City Of The Hindus in Ancient and Modern Times,* Low Price Publications, Delhi. First published in 1868.

Shukla, U.K., 2010, 'Ganga (Varanasi) in Geological Perspective', Paper presented in

Interdisciplinary Seminar on Myths and Scientific studies Nov. 02, 2010, Banaras Hindu University, Varanasi.

Tripathi, Karunapati (ed.), 1991, *Maharshi Vyaspraneetah Sriskandamahapuranantargat Kashikhanda (Parts I, II and III)*, Ganganatha Jha Granthamala, Vol. 13, Sampurnanand Sanskrit University, Varanasi.

Vaidya, C.V., 1986, *History of Sanskrit Literature*, Vol. I *Shruti (Vedic) Period*, Parimal Publications, Delhi.

Winternitz, Maurice, 1987 (reprint), *A History of Indian Literature*, Vol. I, *Introduction, Vedas, Epics, Puranas and Tantras*, A new authoritative translation from original German by V. Srinivasa Sharma, Motilal Banarasidass, Delhi.

8

Varanasi and the Ganga River: A Geological Perspective

U. K. Shukla

INTRODUCTION

The Indo-Gangetic Basin is the largest alluvial tract in the world. Its origin is related to Himalayan building activity which was initiated about 19 Ma ago and is still continued, causing slow but continuous rise of Himalayas in response to compression generated by collision between Indian and Asian plates (Lyon-Caen and Molnar 1985; DeCelles 1998). In response to the temporal rise in the Himalayas, the foreland basin has expanded southwards and rivers shifted due to channel migration and avulsion processes speeded by changing palaeo-climate and base level through Quaternary times (Singh and Bajpai 1989; Shukla and Raju 2008). The basement of the basin is uneven, dissected by a number of lineaments, faults and structural highs that controlled the basin fill history (Sastri et al. 1971; Rao 1973). The basin is filled with sediments eroded mainly from the Himalayas, with some added sediments from the peninsular India. Similarly major water budget (about 70%) to basin is from Himalayas and rest is from craton side. From west to east, the Indo-Gangetic Basin is divisible into Punjab-Rajasthan Plain, Ganga Plain, Bengal Plain and Brahmaputra Plain, respectively.

Centrally located Ganga Plain (77°-88° E longitudes and 24°-30° N latitudes) is highly diversified, showing alluvial geomorphic features of various scales formed in response to climate and tectonic events of the late Quaternary (Fig. 8.1). Because of rich flora and fauna and easy availability of water, the Ganga Plain has been the preferential site for human settlement since the Stone Age. However, large-scale human migration took place only from 3500–3000 BP, which produced a pronounced effect on the land topography (Tiwari et al. 2002). Archaeological sites yielding vertebrate faunal remains and artefacts have been recovered at different places along the Ganga River in Kanpur, Banda, Jalaun, Allahabad and Varanasi Districts of Uttar Pradesh and Bhagalpur in Bihar (Dean 1833; Mishra 2001).

The present study area in Varanasi District is located just 50-60 km away from Vindhyan ranges, which forms the southern limit of the Ganga Plain. This region has been investigated for sedimentology and geomorphic details in a time framework using OSL dating technique to understand the behaviour of the river Ganga and its relationship with Varanasi which is the oldest living city in the world. Survey of India toposheet on different scales, imageries and extensive field surveys helped understanding the geomorphic set-up and river confluence dynamics. It is believed that ancient settlement patterns in and around Varanasi have been greatly influenced by the behaviour of the Ganga River and its tributaries. All these rivers seem to have promptly responded to changing climate, tectonics and sea level related base level changes.

GEOMORPHOLOGY OF THE GANGA PLAIN

The Ganga Plain is located under subtropical humid climate with alternating rainy (monsoon) season, cold season and hot dry season. During monsoon season, more than 80% rainfall occurs due to south-west monsoon system. It is only during the rainy season when large-scale sediment transport occurs in rivers and for rest of the months river channels become almost ponded without any dynamic fluvial activity. This seasonality started right in the Middle Miocene with the rise of the Himalayas to their present heights and have played key role in shaping the geomorphic features of the Ganga Plain.

Geomorphologically, the Ganga Plain is divided into three regions (Fig. 8.1). The Piedmont Plain (Singh 1996; Shukla 2009), located adjacent to Himalayan orogen, shows upliftment and tilting of post-Siwalik

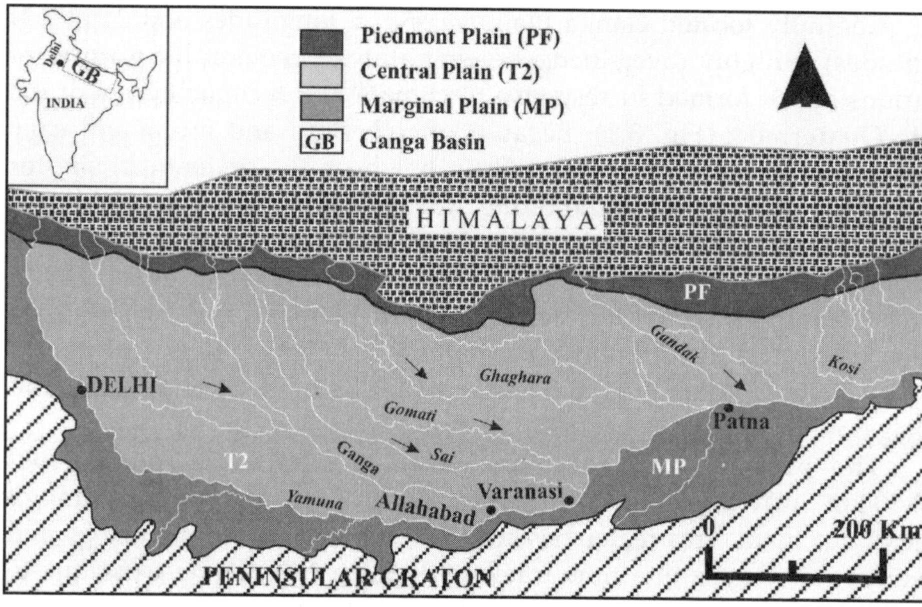

Fig. 8.1. Central Ganga Plain (Basin) bounded by Himalaya in the north and Peninsular Craton in the south shows three major geomorphic subdivisions (PF, T_2 and MP) (modified after Singh, 1996). Major Himalayan rivers and their tributaries are flowing north to southeast, while rivers from the Craton are flowing northwards. The Ganga River is the axial river acting as the water divide between Himalayan and Cratonic rivers.

deposits, conjugate system of strike slip faults, linear ridges, undulating topography and incised rivers. The Central Alluvial Plain shows preferred alignment of river channels with prominent tectonic trends of NW-SE and WNW-ESE (Singh et al., 1996; Shukla and Raju 2008). Kilometre-scale warping of the surface is prominent. The Marginal Alluvial Plain exhibits incision of river channels, kilometre-scale geomorphic highs, conjugate set of fractures, bending, up-doming, tilted blocks, and triangular facets in the cliff sections (Singh et al. 1997). In the cratonward margin E-W and SW-NE trending faults and lineaments are related to the activation of pre-existing lineaments in the cratonic basement (Singh 2004), though some of them developed during the Quaternary and are confined to alluvium only. The existing lineaments have largely controlled the river courses and are often occupied by the river valleys.

Rather flat-looking Ganga Plain has a gentle southeasterly slope followed by numerous Himalayan and alluvium-fed rivers (Fig. 8.1). The Ganga is the trunk river of the Ganga Plain, about 2225 km long, it emanates from Gangotri glacier in the Himalayas and passing through vast alluvial plains makes a huge delta system in the Bay of Bengal and supplies sediment load to the deep sea fan. The Ganga gains its name at Devprayag in the Uttarakhand Himalaya, where Bhagirathi and Alakananda Rivers meet to form the main Ganga River channel (Fig. 8.2). All the major and the minor rivers in the Ganga Plain are incised into the regional Upland Terrace Surface (T_2 Surface), and flowing on the T_0 surface, show the development of River Valley Terrace Surface (T_1 Surface) (Fig. 8.3). In the western Ganga Plain, Yamuna acts as the axial river up to Allahabad where it meets with Ganga, and in the eastern part, Ganga is the axial river. The Ganga River in the eastern Ganga Plain makes the water divide between the northern plains formed of Himalayan derived grey-coloured mica rich sediments, subgreywacke in composition and southern plains produced by reddish-coloured sediments derived from Peninsular India, characterised by non-micaceous subarkosic sediments (Shukla and Raju 2008). The Ganga foreland basin was filled by fluvial

Fig. 8.2. Bhagirathi and Alaknanda Rivers meet at Devprayag in Uttarakhand state to form the Ganga River. Bhagirathi waters are turbid due to Tehri Dam in the upstream reaches.

processes depositing huge sediment loads eroded from Himalayas in the north and some sediment from Peninsular Craton in the south (Fig. 8.1).

THE GANGA RIVER AT VARANASI

The Ganga River drains a 10,60,000 km^2 basin that covers over 25% of India's total surface area between Himalayan foothills in the north to Peninsular Craton in the south (Rao 1975). From its source to the sea, the river is intimately related to civilisation since ancient times. The Ganga, all along its length, flows through a well-defined valley which is generally 2–20 km wide. The active Ganga River channel and its narrow floodplain are incised in the River Valley Terrace Surface (T_1) developed within the

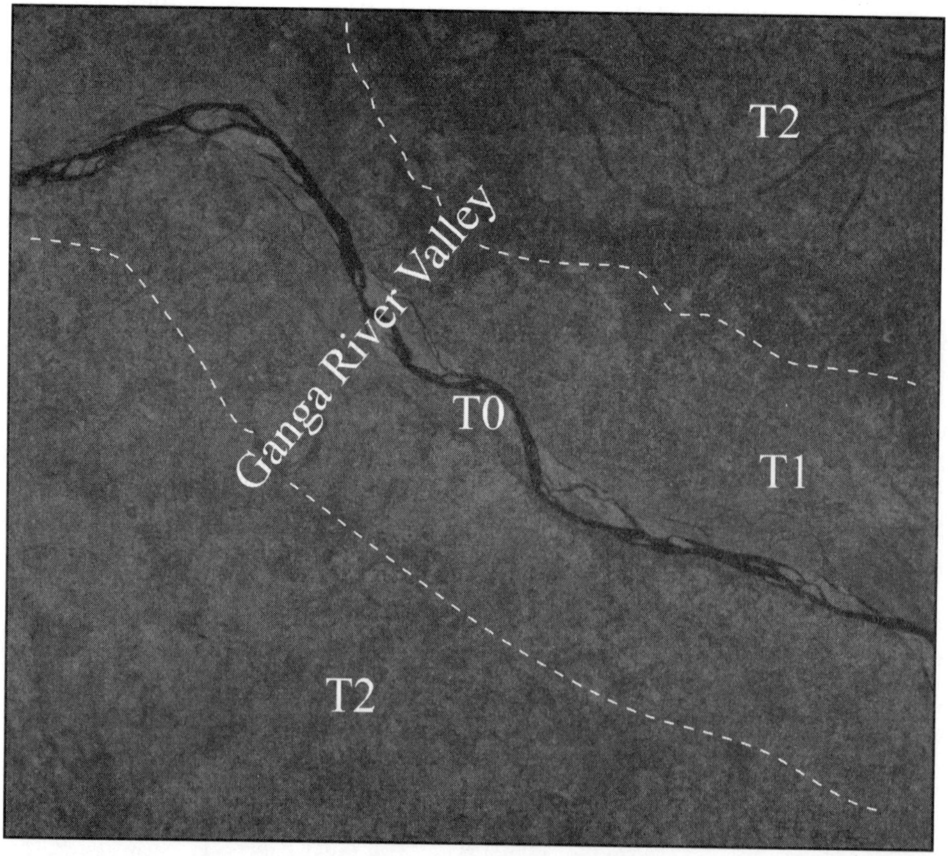

Fig. 8.3. Land Sat imageries of upstream of Allahabad showing braided Ganga River and associated flood plains (T_0 surface), River Valley Terrace (T_1 surface) and the oldest Upland Terrace Surface (T_2 surface) exhibiting abandoned channel belt on the right upper corner.

river valley (Shukla et al., 2001). The Ganga River Valley margin is well defined and bordered by cliffs of variable heights (8-30 m high) made up of Upland Terrace Surface (T_2) sediments (Fig. 8.3). The Ganga shows distinctive changes in valley morphology, channel characteristics, hydraulic regime sediment load along its length, and has been divided into seven segments (M. Singh et al. 2007; Singh 2008).

The region between Allahabad and Buxar is designated as GRV–III (M. Singh et al. 2007). From Allahabad downstream after confluence with the Yamuna, the Ganga becomes the axial river of the Ganga Plain (Fig. 8.1). Many important tributaries, namely Varuna, Gomati, Ghaghra, Gandak and Kosi from north and Tons, Son, Punpun, Phalgu, Jirgo and many other rivers join the Ganga from south. Around Varanasi city, Ganga is the principal river flowing incised into its narrow valley (1-2 km wide) from south to northeast direction. Ganga makes a prominent

Fig. 8.4. Photograph showing steep cliff along the Ganga River over which Ramnagar Township is located (see inset). River is flowing towards NE. Excavated profile at Oriya Ghat of the Ramnagar cliff section two sedimentary packages I (pink coloured, Craton derived; and dated as 40 ka) and II (grey coloured, Himalayan sediments; dated at the top as 7 ka) are distinct and at the top are capped by cultural layers.

meander loop having cut side towards Varanasi (Shukla and Raju 2008; Srivastava and Shukla 2009). On the opposite side a wide point bar is developed followed by a vertical cliff along the valley margin on which Ramnagar town is located (Fig. 8.4). Here, the Ganga has two tributaries, namely Assi *nala* (river) on the southern flank and Varuna River in the north eastern side of the city. Both the rivers are presently incised cutting into older alluvium also called as Bangar.

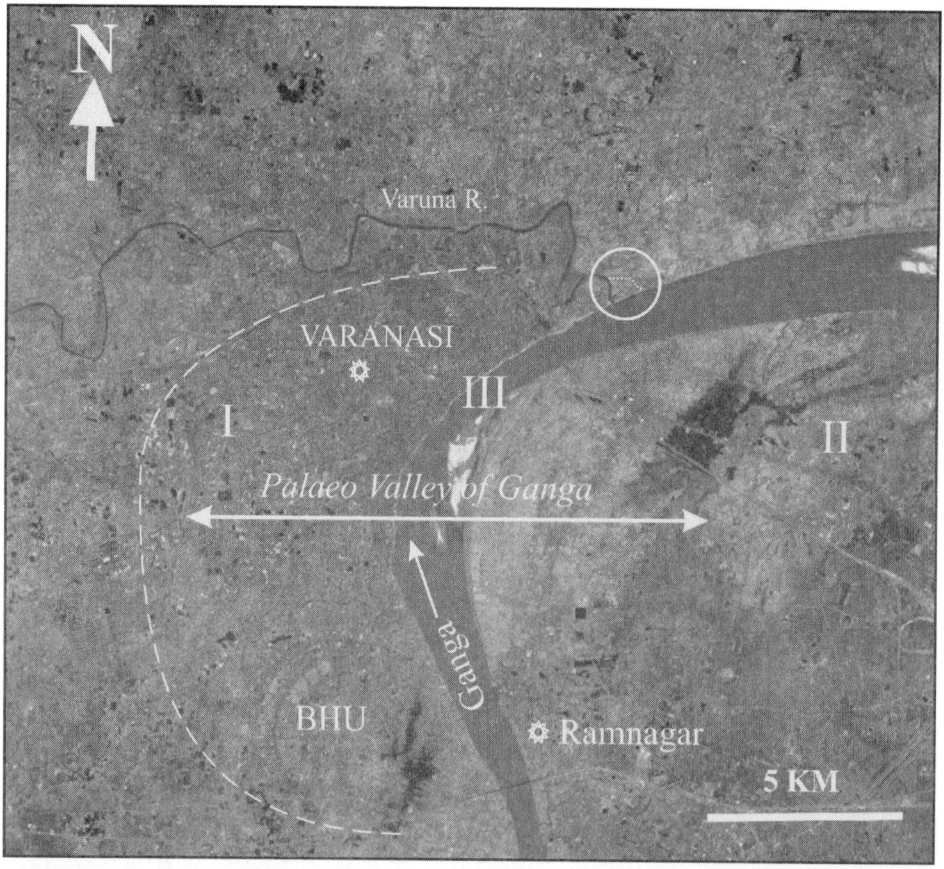

Fig. 8.5. Imagery showing present-day Ganga River confined within its narrow valley, and its much wider palaeovalley (12-15 km wide) when it was not incised and freely migrating from position I to II and finally back to its present location III. City of Varanasi is located on the older floodplain of the Ganga River encircled by white broken line. Within the city, a number of ponds are visible in black colour. Also, note the confluence point of Varuna with Ganga; it has shifted from north (white dotted circle) to its present confluence about half a kilometre in the south.

CONFLUENCE DYNAMICS OF GANGA RIVER AND ITS TRIBUTARIES

In the segment GRV – III between Allahabad to Buxar, the Ganga River Valley is rather narrow, flows over the basement high (Vindhyan Plateau). At the beginning, the river flows east up to Chunar, where basement rocks are exposed. Between Chunar and Buxar, the river flows NE, which is the direction of basement lineament. The river channel is sinuous and shifting from one margin of the valley to the other. Mostly, cliffs are present on both the margins of the valley, though in few areas cliff is present only on southern side of the valley.

To understand the confluence behaviour of tributaries with the Ganga River channel, three tributaries, namely the Gomati and Varuna Rivers, meeting from north and the Jirgo River and a few smaller tributaries joining Ganga channel from south (near Chunar), respectively, have been studied using toposheets and imageries. It appears that the confluence points of

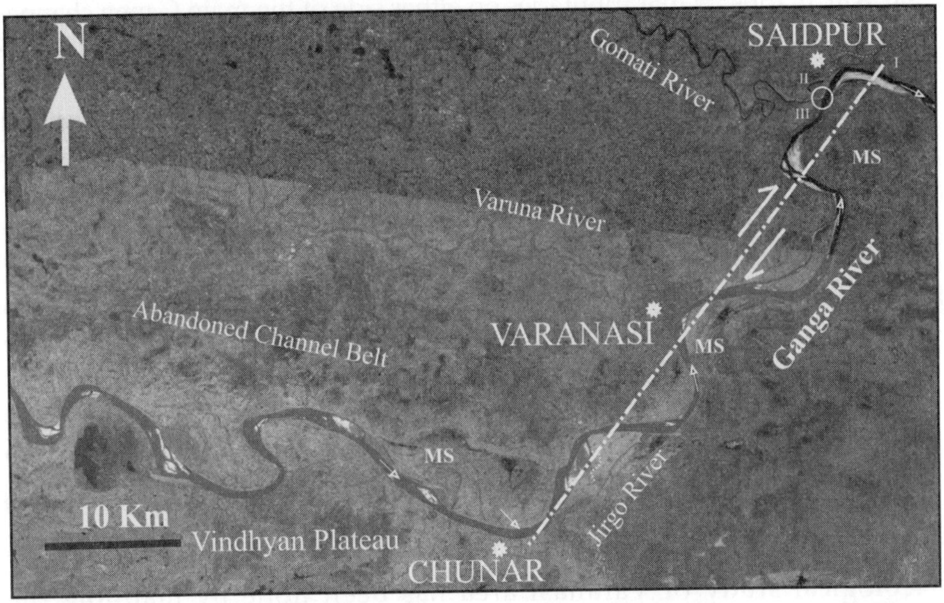

Fig. 8.6. Imagery photograph showing the nature of the Ganga River in sector GRV-III, and a fault showing right handed strike slip movement along the Ganga River between Chunar and Saidpur. At Chunar, the river takes the U-turn and starts flowing to NE. It shows a very narrow valley and distorted meanders. Northern tributaries such as Gomati River shows a progressive southward shift of its confluence with the Ganga from position I to II and III which is its present confluence point. The Varuna River also shows the same tendency (see Fig. 5). Southern tributary, the Jirgo River, also shows confluence shift from south (dotted line) to north. MS stands for abandoned meander scars present on either side of the Ganga River channel. Up current of Chunar, a prominent abandoned channel belt is present.

both the northern tributaries have shifted progressively southwards in discrete steps, whereas confluences of southern rivers tend to shift towards north, leaving behind abandoned channel belts (Figs. 8.5 and 8.6). However, shift of confluence points seems related to dynamics of the main channel of the river Ganga. Probably sometimes during the late Quaternary, rivers were not incised, and were freely migrating and shifting laterally, within their broad valleys for many kilometres. Lateral migration of the Ganga is clearly evidenced by the presence of huge meander scars on either side of the present course of Ganga. Prominent abandoned meander scars can be seen, for instance, near Saidpur, which is the junction point of Gomati River, at Varanasi near the confluence of the Varuna River and, at Chunar where river Jirgo joins Ganga from south. When compared with these abandoned meander scars, the meanders of the Ganga River appear distorted and stretched having straight and highly convoluted reaches indicating a tectonic control on the present-day river channel (Fig. 8.6). It appears that tributaries on either side of the main Ganga channel tried to adopt the shortest route made available by the lateral shift of the Ganga itself.

Near Varanasi, where presently due to incision the Ganga is confined within a 1-2 km wide narrow valley, earlier it had a much wider valley which was 10-15 km wide (Fig. 8.5). With time it had migrated eastward leaving behind a huge abandoned meander belt on which the oldest city of Varanasi is located. The location of Varanasi represents the older flood plain of the Ganga. Finally, the Ganga River again shifted westward to its present location and got incised within the River Valley Terrace Surface (T_1 surface) forming high cliff towards Ramnagar township and a gradually rising terrace surface towards Varanasi. The incision of the Ganga seems related to tectonics along a fault line passing in NE-SW direction and also controlling the course of the river (Shukla and Raju 2008).

GEOLOGY OF VARANASI

Geological study of Varanasi area has been done by mapping the Ramnagar cliff section and documenting various pits dug for archeological investigation in Ramnagar and Akhta areas located at the periphery of the city. Available borehole data has been integrated with the outcrop information to understand the Ganga River migration, its channel characteristics and sedimentary fill of its valley through Quaternary times. Samples were collected for OSL (Optically Stimulated

Thermoluminescence) dating for interpreting the geological evolution of the study area in a time framework.

RAMNAGAR CLIFF SECTION

The cliff section exposed for about 750 m at the Ramnagar has been studied by vertical and lateral profiling and is OSL dated. The cliff section is 12 to 20 m thick and composed of diverse lithology that can be grouped into two distinct Sedimentary Packages I and II, based on nature of the sand/ mud horizons (Fig. 8.4). The older Sedimentary Succession I, occurring at the base of all the profiles, shows a variable thickness of 1 to 6 m (average 4 m). The succession is made up of pinkish yellow non-micaceous arkosic sands and related silt-clay units, which is similar to sand being brought by modern rivers flowing northwards carrying sediments from southern craton. Capped by a 50-70 cm thick sheet like laterally persistent greyish mud horizon, in general, the Sedimentary Package I is fining upward in character. The litho-units show a variety of primary physical features indicating deposition by river channels. The capping mud horizon is dated as 39.3±5.4 ka (Srivastava and Shukla 2009).

The younger overlying Sedimentary Package II is separated by a sharp and erosional contact from the older Sedimentary Package I (Fig. 8.4). It seems that after deposition of older sedimentary package, the surface was briefly eroded to produce an undulatory surface. In contrast to the reddish brown craton-derived sediments of the older Sedimentary Package I, the younger one is made up of grey, micaceous Himalayan derived sediments. In general, it is characterised by alternation of channelized sand and mud units suggesting sedimentation in smaller tributary-like rivers that would have been meeting with the main Ganga channel from north. This younger sedimentary package is dated at the top just below the cultural unit as 7±1 ka (Srivastava and Shukla 2009). Top of this natural sedimentary succession is capped by a 5-10 m thick cultural layer having the pre-NBP pottery and other artefacts dating back to *c.* 3000 BP.

Characteristically, the sedimentary succession exposed at Ramnagar cliff shows structural deformation exhibiting features such as faults, folds, and inclined bed sets, near vertical to inclined fractures filled with sparry calcite and liquefaction structures. All these structural features suggest that the study area suffered neotectonic events, probably associated with seismic pulses, during sedimentation.

Interestingly, both the above-mentioned Sedimentary Packages I and II comprising craton-derived sediments erosionally followed by Himalayan sediments respectively, are also encountered in boreholes dug within Varanasi city at DLW (Diesel Locomotive Workshop), Gurubagh and Chowk. They are several tens of metres to more than hundred metres thick and interbedded in the subsurface stratigraphy. In each of the boreholes, top 30–50 m is represented by mud horizons.

DISCUSSION

Field evidence, geomorphology and sedimentology of Varanasi area show that in the present-day situation, any river bringing sediments from craton side cannot cross the channel of the Ganga River and deposit it on the Varanasi side. Similarly, no river from Himalyan side can deposit the sediment south of Ganga (Figs. 8.1, 8.5 and 8.6). However, as evidenced by the presence of craton-derived sediments in the Ramnagar cliff located north-east of Ganga (Fig. 8.4), and in boreholes within the Varanasi city located south-west of the Ganga (Shukla and Rajau 2008, Figs. 3, 4), it becomes evident that sometimes during the late Quaternary, the Ganga was not present at its present location in Varanasi. It came near Varanasi about 40 ka BP, and before that it was vigorously oscillating within its palaeovalley quickly changing its channel position (Shukla and Raju, 2008; Srivastava and Shukla 2009) (Figs. 8.5 and 8.6). This provided opportunity to rivers flowing both from north and south to interact, and the craton-derived sediments were carried by the rivers to Ramnagar and beyond. Further, the older Sedimentary Package I shows tectonic features such as fault, folds, cracks and synsedimentary liquefaction indicating to a major tectonic event. It appears that the Ganga shifted to Varanasi in response to this event only at about 40 ka BP. This tectonic event is also recorded from Kalpi section exposed along the Yamuna river about 350 km away from Varanasi (Singh et al. 1997; Tiwari et al. 2002). The tectonic event responsible for the shift of the river Ganga in Varanasi, therefore, appears to be a major tectonic turmoil that affected a good part of the Ganga Basin.

The lateral migration of the river Ganga and its tributaries is well displayed in the form of meander scars and abandoned channel belts visible in the imageries (Figs. 8.5 and 8.6). Before coming to its present location, the Ganga had a wide valley and it was shifting within its valley and changed its position many a time between 40 ka and 7 ka. During this time period many smaller rivers carrying the Himalayan derived sediments would have been coming up to Varanasi and deposited the younger Sedimentary Package II. The Ganga came to its present location at about 7 ka BP and got incised in response to another tectonic event that deformed both the sedimentary packages I and II exposed the Ramnagar cliff section (Fig. 8.4). Once the cliff was formed, it started degrading by gullying activity, and it continued at least for 4000 years, before the human settlement in Ramnagar area took place at about 3000 years ago (Jayaswal and Kumar 2005-6; Jayaswal 2006-7).

Based on NE trend of the Ganga River, its distorted meanders, narrow valley and the differential disposition of craton-derived sediments on the surface in the Ramnagar cliff and deep into subsurface in different boreholes within the Varanasi across the course of the river, Shukla and Raju (2008) indicated that near Varanasi, the Ganga is flowing along a fault. The confluence dynamics of Gomati, Varuna and Jirgo within the Sector DRV-III, further corroborates the view and also indicates that the nature of the fault is dextral strike slip with a gravity component, where Ramnagar side is upthrown block and Varanasi side is downthrown block (Fig. 8.6).

CONCLUSION

1. The Ganga River came near Varanasi at around 40 ka BP, and to its present location at about 7 ka BP. Between 40 ka and 7 ka, the river was vigorously shifting its channel position rendering the area unsuitable for any type of anthropogenic activity. And probably because of this reason, unlike other areas of Ganga Plain where settlement started during late Pleistocene (Palaeolithic) and early Holocene (Mesolithic to Neolithic) times, Varanasi region was inhabited much later (around 3500–3000 BP). This is because the river got stranded due to incision following a tectonic event at 7 ka BP. The tectonic upheaval appears to result in raised surfaces, a particular suitable habitat for human settlement.
2. Varanasi is located on the older floodplain of the Ganga River, which is attested by the numerous ponds formed due to the abandonment of palaeochannels.
3. Between Chunar and Saidpur, the Ganga river is flowing NE along a dextral (right handed) strike slip fault, having a gravity

component, where Ramnagar side is upthrown block and Varanasi side is a downthrown block.

4. Geomorphologic studies of the present type, besides unveiling paleo-landscape and history of water channels, may also throw significant light in the quest of scientific approval or disapproval of the myths associated with the oldest living city of Varanasi and its intimacy with the Ganga, which is addressed in mythology as the 'mother' and the 'goddess', etc.

ACKNOWLEDGEMENTS

Author is thankful to the Head of the Centre of Advanced study in Geology, BHU, for providing the working facilities of the Department. Dr. Kuldeep Prakash is thanked for discussion and sharing a few photographs for the study.

REFERENCES

Dean, E., 1833, 'Notes on the specimen of the Kankar Formation, and on the Fossils Bones Collected on the Jamna', *Journal of the Asiatic Society of Bengal* 2: 622-635.

DeCelles, P.G., G.E. Gehrels, J. Quade, T.P. Ojha, P.A. Kapp and B.N. Upreti, 1998, 'Neogene Foreland Basin Deposits, Erosional Unroofing, and the Kinematic History of the Himalayan Fold-thrust Belt, Western Nepal', *Geological Society of America Bulletin* 110: 2-21.

Jayaswal, V. and M. Kumar, 2005-6, 'Excavations at Ramnagar: Discovery of Supporting Settlement of Ancient Varanasi', *Puratattva* 36: 85-92.

Jayaswal, V., 2006-7, Ramnagar Excavations: 2007, *Jnana-Pravaha Bulletin No. 10*: 237-240.

Lyon-Caen, H. and P. Molnar, 1985, 'Gravity Anomalies, Flexure of Indian Plate and the Structure, Support and Evolution of Himalaya and Ganga Basin', *Tectonics* 4: 513-538.

Mishra, V.P., 2001, 'Significance of Quaternary Vertebrates from Gangetic Alluvium', *Special Publication: Geological Society of India* 65(III): 195-198.

Rao, M.B.R., 1973, 'The subsurface geology of Indo-Gangetic Plains', *Journal of Geological Society of India* 14: 217-242.

Sastri, V.V., L.L. Bhandari, A.T.R. Raju and A.K. Dutta, 1971, 'Tectonic Framework and Subsurface Stratigraphy of the Ganga Basin', *Journal of Geological Society of India* 12: 222-233.

Shukla, U.K., I.B. Singh, M. Sharma and S. Sharma, 2001, 'A Model of Alluvial Megafan Sedimentation: Ganga Megafan', *Sedimentary Geology* 144: 243-262.

Shukla, U.K. and N.J. Raju, 2008, 'Migration of the Ganga River and Its Implications on Hydro-Geological Potential of Varanasi Area, U. P., India', *Journal of Earth System Science* 117: 489-498.

Shukla, U.K., 2009, 'Sedimentation Model of Gravel-Dominated Alluvial Piedmont Fan, Ganga Plain, India', *International Journal of Earth Sciences (Geol Rundsch)* 98: 443-459.

Singh, I.B. and V.N. Bajpai, 1989, 'Significance of Syndepositional Tectonics in the Facies Development of Ganga Alluvium near Kanpur, U.P.', *Journal of Geological Society of India* 34: 61-66.

Singh, I.B., 1996, 'Geological Evolution of Ganga Plain-An Overview', *Journal of Palaeontological Society of India* 41: 99-137.

Singh, I.B., A.A. Ansari, R.S. Chandel and A. Mishra, 1996, 'Neotectonic Control on Drainage System in Gangetic Plain, Uttar Pradesh', *Journal of Geological Society of India* 47: 599-609.

Singh, I.B., G. Rajagopalan, K.K. Agarwal, P. Srivastava, M. Sharma and S. Sharma, 1997, 'Evidence of Middle to Late Holocene Neotectonic Activity in the Ganga Plain', *Current Science* 73: 1114-1117.

Singh, I.B., 2004, 'Late Quaternary History of the Ganga Plain', *Journal of Geological Society of India* 64: 431-454.

Singh, I.B., 2008, 'The Ganga River', in A. Gupta (ed.), *Large Rivers Geomorphology and Management*, Willey: 347-371.

Singh, M., I.B. Singh and G. Müller, 2007, 'Sediment Characteristics and Transportation Dynamics of the Ganga River', *Geomorphology* 86: 144-175.

Srivastava, P. and U.K. Shukla, 2009. 'Quaternary Evolution of the Ganga River System: New Quartz Ages and a Review of Luminescence Chronology', *Himalayan Geology* 30: 85-94.

Tiwari, R., P.C. Pant, I.B. Singh, S. Sharma, M. Sharma, P. Srivastava, A.K. Singhvi, P.K. Mishra and H.J. Tobschall, 2002, 'Middle Palaeolithic Human Activity and Palaeoclimate at Kalpi in Yamuna Valley, Ganga Plain', *Man and Environment* XXVI: 1-13.

9

Gaṅgā and Kāśī: Myths and Scientific Enquiries

Meera Sharma

River Gaṅgā to an Indian mind is not just a water channel of geographical physique, but is a symbol of a long culture make-up which has been nurtured by religious faith. For *Banarasis* (inhabitants of Varanasi), Gaṅgā is the lifeline of Kāśī-culture. Ancient Indian texts reflect this distinctively through narrative descriptions. It is, therefore, not surprising that all the aspects of this 'divine river'—origin, long path of its flow, falling into the ocean, cities and regions served by its channel, etc., form theme of mythological stories, which are numerous in literature. Purāṇas in particular are mine of these stories, in which Gaṅgā, Śiva and Kāśī go hand in hand and occur many a time. The *Pauranic* concept, Śiva, Kāśī and Gaṅgā are inseparable, and is so deep-rooted that one can often find people saying such folk phrase as—

चना चबेना गंग जल, जो पुजवें करतार। काशी कबहूँ न छोड़िये, विश्वनाथ दरबार।

(Kāśī, the court of Lord Śiva, should never be abandoned, even if one subsists on most meagre food (grams) and water of the river Gaṅgā).

Kāśī is said to have the reputation of being the oldest city, and a very holy pilgrimage, while Gaṅgā is addressed as a goddess. There are, however, references in the literature which indicate that there was a pre-Gaṅgā stage in Kāśī region. Motichandra, for instance, had sensed this stage as a probability. But, he left this significant issue unresolved by saying that—"Indeed Kāśī and Gaṅgā are inseparable. But, whether numerous cliffs and mounds so characteristics of Kāśī region were earlier or the channel of the Gaṅgā, the creator of the morphology of this region was earlier is question of *Deva-yuga* (remote past), which is illogical for us. But, it is apparent that the region lying between Gaṅgā and Gomati plains was created by nature for human settlement, in which Kāśī Janapada was established" (translated Motichandra 2003: 13-14). Pauranic stories mention names of rivers, ponds, tanks and waterbodies, which appear to pre-date the channel of Gaṅgā. These references bring forth two notable factors—one that in pre-Gaṅgā stage, Kāśī region had plenty of water resources, and two, the advent of the perennial water channel of Gaṅgā in this region was an important event, which remained in the memory of the people.

The present paper, therefore, proposes to scrutinise mythological stories narrating Kāśī and Gaṅgā with the aim to ascertain the historicity of waterbodies, particularly the channel of the river Gaṅgā in Kāśī. Pauranic stories like *Gaṅgā-avataraṇa* (advent of the river Gaṅgā), for instance suggest that Gaṅgā started flowing in the plain from one specific time, which has been addressed as 'advent', one of the very significant events of ancient Kāśī. All important descriptions related to the *Gaṅgā-avtaraṇa,* have been arranged within a chronological frame, which will help in noting the development of this mythology, as well as ascertaining the probable historicity of the events, for which chronology of ancient Indian literature is important to note.

The date and chronology of the ancient Indian texts is a controversial issue. The commonly accepted dates and chronology of the select compositions, which receive focus in this paper, have been summarised. The earliest literary composition, the *Ṛgveda*, is dated around 2000–2500 BCE (Witernitz, M. 1987: 288; Pant, P.C. and Renu Bala. 1993: 104). *Śatapatha Brāhmaṇa*, which has been placed between the composition of *Ṛgveda Saṁhitā* and the origin of Buddhism, is supposed to have been compiled around 1200–1000 BCE (Pande, G.C. 2001: 430; Witernitz, M. 1987: 288). The epic *Rāmāyaṇa* is dated to *c.* 3rd/4th century BCE, while *Mahābhārata* between 400 BCE and 400 CE (Witernitz, M. 1987: 288). The Pauranic literature has much wider time span, as it dates between *c.* 1st and

15th/16th centuries CE (Witernitz, M. 1987: 288; Banerjee, S.C. 1991: 12; Hazra, R.C. 1987: 174-189). The above-mentioned texts, covering a wide time bracket, are full of mythological stories, in which Gaṅgā and Kāśī also fair well. It is proposed to discuss some of the descriptions of the texts maintaining the chronology of its source, the text.

Gaṅgā in the Vedic Literature

The earliest reference of the river Gaṅgā perhaps is the following passage of the 6th Maṇḍala of *Ṛgveda* (Pande, G.C. 2001: 45; Pant, P.C. 1993: 104).

अधि बृबुः पणीनां वर्षिष्ठे मूर्धन्नस्थात्।
उरूः कक्षो न गाङ्ग्यः (6.45.31)

(Similar to the high cliffs of Gaṅgā, Bribu was established in the middle region of Pāṇī) (Sharma, Shriram. 2008: 918).

According to Pande, the word *Kaksha* denotes the bank, or the region on the bank of the river Gaṅgā (Pande, G.C. 2001: 45-46).

The 10th Maṇḍala of *Ṛgveda* gives a long list of rivers in the compostion of Nadī-sūkta (10.75.56), which starts with Gaṅgā and reads as below:

इमं मे गङ्गे यमुने सरस्वती शुतुद्रि स्तोमं सचता पुरूष्ण्या।
असिक्न्या मरूद्वृधे वितस्तयाऽऽर्जीकीये शृणुह्या सुषोमया।।

(Ho! Rivers Gaṅgā, Yamunā, Saraswatī, Purūṣni, Asiknī ... after dividing my stream within your shares you listen to my prayer) (Sharma, Sriram. 2008: 918).

Pande notes that the list of the rivers of Nadī-sūkta in the order of east to west may be interpreted in terms of the flow of the river Gaṅgā in the plain, and the importance of the eastern region (Pande, G.C. 2001: 45).

Gaṅgā occurs in *Śatapatha Brāhmaṇa* as part of the story of Bharata Dushyanti, according to which when king Dushyanti was performing *yajña* he tied for *vṛttahantā* 75 horses at the bank of Yamunā and 55 horses near Gaṅgā (Eggeling, Julius 1990: 399. 13.5.4.11).

The above account suggests that, though the earliest reference of the river Gaṅgā occurs in the *Ṛgveda* (6.45.31, and 10.75.56), the mythology of *Gaṅgā-avtaraṇa* was not formulated by this time. It appears that, during Vedic period Gaṅgā was not of much significance. It was just a river like others—the Indus and the Sarswatī.

Gaṅgā in the Epic Literature

First detailed description of Gaṅgā—its origin, expansion and geography, along with its religious significance—is found in the epics. Both *Rāmāyaṇa* (1.39.4–5, 21; 1.40.4–30; 1.42.1–10) and *Mahābhārata* (Bhīṣmaparva 6.28.47) not only portray the river as divine, but its origin too has been said to be with god's grace. Viśwāmitra, while narrating the story of origin and expansion of the river Gaṅgā to Rama, says (*Rāmāyaṇa* 1.35.14-17):

शैलेन्द्रो हिमवान् राम धातुनामाकरो महान्।.... ।। 14 ।।
या मेरूदुहिता राम तयोर्माता सुमध्यमा।
नाम्ना मेना मनोज्ञा वै पत्नी हिमवतः प्रिया।। 15 ।।
तस्यां गंगेयमभवज्ज्येष्ठा हिमवतः सुता।.... ।। 16 ।।
यथ ज्येष्ठां सुराः सर्वे देवकार्यचिकीर्षया।
शैलेन्द्रं वरयामासुर्गंगा त्रिपथगां नदीम्।। 17 ।।

(Gaṅgā is the elder daughter of the Himālaya, the king of mountains, and Mainā, the daughter of Meru mountain. After some time gods, for the performance of divine activities, asked the king of mountains, Himalaya, to give them his eldest daughter, who descended from the heaven in the form of three-streamed river) (Hindi translation by Pandeya, R. S. 1996: 102).

This passage clearly suggests that the Gaṅgā was initially a river of the Himalyan region. Its flow in the plain was a later geological event. As, according to the *Gaṅgā-avataraṇa* myth of *Rāmāyaṇa* (1.42.1-13), Gaṅgā descended to revive 60,000 sons of the King Sagara, who were burnt to ashes due to the curse of Kapila Muni.

भगीरथस्तु....................................... ।। 11 ।।
मन्त्रिष्वाधाय तद् राज्यं गंगावतरणे रतः।
तपो दीर्घं समातिष्ठद् गोकर्णे रघुनन्दन।। 12 ।।
....तस्य वर्षसहस्त्राणि घोरे तपसि तिष्ठतः।। 13 ।।

(For the descend of Gaṅgā, King Bhagīratha, leaving responsibility of protection of his kingdom and the people to the ministers, performed penance on the Gokarṇa mountain. He spent 1000 years in savior penance) (Hindi translation by Pandeya, R. S. 1996:114).

Lord Brahmā, the creator, was pleased, and asked the king to ask for a *varadāna* (blessing) (*Rāmāyaṇa* 1.42.14-22). When the king asked for the blessing, Brahmā said:

इयं हैमवती ज्येष्ठा गंगा हिमवतः सुता।
तां वै धारयितुं राजन् हरस्तत्र नियुज्यताम्।। 23।।

(She is Haimāvatī Gaṅgā, the eldest daughter of Himālaya. Request Lord Śiva to retain her) (Hindi translation by Pandeya, R. S. 1996: 114).

Gaṅgā is addressed here as 'Haimāvatī', which appears to suggest that the river at that point of time was in the form of a glacier. Śiva became happy by Bhagīratha's one year penance, and agreed to hold Gaṅgā on his head (*Rāmāyaṇa 1.43.1-3;* Hindi translation by Pandeya, R.S. 1996: 115).

ततो हैमवती ज्येष्ठा सर्वलोकनमस्कृता।
तदा सातिमहद्रूपं कृत्वा वेगं च दुःसहम्।। 4।।
आकाशादपतद् राम शिवे शिवशिरस्युत।

(The elder daughter of Himālaya, Gaṅgā, who is bowed by all the world, transformed into a large size fell with unbearable velocity on the bright head of the Lord Śiva) (*Rāmāyaṇa 1.431-3;* Hindi translation by Pandeya, R.S. 1996: 114).

The hair locks (*jaṭā*) of Śiva are described as below:

हिमवत्प्रतिमे राम जटामण्डलगह्वरे।.... ।। 8।।
नैव सा निर्गमं लेभे जटामण्डलमन्ततः।
तत्रैवाबभ्रमद् देवी संवत्सरगणान् बहून ।। 9।।

(..His forehead adorned by hairlocks appears to be similar to Himalayas with a cave. Gaṅgā kept wondering in the hairlocks of Lord Śiva for many years, as she could not trace a path to get out of it) (Hindi translation by Pandeya, R.S. 1996: 115).

King Bhagīratha again performed penance as a result of which Gaṅgā was brought and left at Bindu-sarovara by Śiva, where it got separated into seven channels (*Rāmāyaṇa* 1.43.11):

विससर्ज ततो गंगां हरो बिन्दुसरः प्रति।
तस्यां विसृज्यमानायां सप्त स्त्रोतांसि जज्ञिरे।। 11।।
ह्लादिनी पावनी चैव नलिनी च तथैव च।
तिस्त्रः प्राचीं दिशं जग्मुर्गंगाः शिवजलाः शुभाः।। 12।।
सुचक्षुश्चैव सीता च सिन्धुश्चैव महानदी।
तिस्त्रश्चैवता दिशं जग्मुः प्रतीचीं तु दिशं शुभा।। 13।।
सप्तमी चान्वगात् तासां भगीरथरथं तदा।
भगीरथोऽपि राजर्षिर्दिव्यं स्यन्दनमास्थितः।। 14।।
प्रायादग्रे महातेजा गंगा तं चाप्यनुव्रजत।.... ।। 15।।

(The three *maṅgalamayī* channels—Hladini, Pavani and Nalini of the Gaṅgā went towards east. While three pious streams—Chakshu, Sita and the great Sindhu began to flow towards western direction. The remaining seventh streams started following the chariot of the King Bhagīratha. Surmounted on the divine chariot the glorious King Bhagīratha led the path, which was followed by Gaṅgā) (Hindi translation by Pandeya, R.S. 1996: 115).

....ततो हि यजमानस्य जह्नोरद्भुतकर्मणः ।। 34 ।।
गंगा सम्प्लावयामास यज्ञवाटं महात्मनः।
तपस्यावलेपनं ज्ञात्वा क्रुद्धो जन्हुश्च राघव।। 35 ।।
अपिबत् तु जलं सर्वं गंगायाः परमाद्भुतम्।

(At that time on their way a very brave king Jāhnu was performing *yajña*. Gaṅgā washed away his *yajña-maṇḍapa*. Raghunandana, King Jāhnu took this event as pride of Gaṅgā, and drank its entire water. This was a wonder for the world) (Hindi translation by Pandeya, R.S. 1996: 116).

ततो देवा.. ।। 36 ।।
पूजयन्ति महात्मानं जह्नुं पुरूषसत्तमम्।... ।। 37 ।।
ततस्तुष्टो महातेजाः श्रोताभ्यामसष्जत् प्रभुः।
तस्माज्जह्नुसुता गंगा प्रोच्यते जाह्नवीति च ।। 38 ।।

(Then gods started praising Mahātmā Jāhnu, which pleased Jāhnu, who released the stream of Gaṅgā through the hole of his ear. Thus Gaṅgā appeared again on the surface, and was known as Jānhavī, the daughter of Jāhnu) (Hindi translation by Pandeya, R.S. 1996: 117).

जगाम च पुनर्गंगा भगीरथरथानुगा।
सागरं चापि सम्प्राप्ता सा सरित्प्रवरा तदा।। 39 ।।
रसातलमुपागच्छत् सिद्धयर्थं तस्य कर्मणः।... ।। 40 ।।

(From there, Gaṅgā again started following the chariot of King Bhagīratha. The supreme river of the rivers, Jānhavī reached the ocean, where in order to bless the forefathers of the King Bhagīratha she went underground) (Hindi translation by Pandeya, R.S. 1996: 117).

This long narration of *Gaṅgā-avataraṇa* of *Rāmāyaṇa* with slight modification also forms part of the epic *Mahābhārata*. Bhīṣmaparva (6.10-29) while describing in detail the *Sudarśana-dvīpa* threw light on *Gaṅgā-avataraṇa*.

परिमण्डलस्तयोर्मध्ये मेरूः कनकपर्वतः।.... ।। 10 ।।
तस्य शैलस्य शिखरात् क्षीरधारा नरेश्वर।

विश्वरूपापरिमिता भीमनिर्घातनिःस्वना।। 28।।
पुण्या पुण्यतमैर्जुष्टा गंगा भागीरथी शुभा।
प्लवन्तीव प्रवेगेन ह्रदे चन्द्रमसः शुभे।। 29।।
तया ह्युत्पादितः पुण्यः स ह्रदः सागरोपमः।
तां धारयामास तदा दुर्धरां पर्वतैरपि।। 30।।
शतं वर्षसहस्त्राणां शिरसैव पिनाकधृक्.... ।। 31।।

(From the peak of circular and golden Meru mountain milky white, strong, thundering and beautiful stream of Bhāgīrathī Gaṅgā fell with great velocity in the circular tank (Bhīṣmaparva 6.10-29; Hindi translation by Pandeya, R.S. 1996: 2556-2558). The pious tank has been carved by the Gaṅgā, which, due to its numerous water source, looks like a sea. Lord Śiva, Pinākadhārī, retained Gaṅgā for one lac years on his forehead, which was difficult to be held even by the mountains) (Bhīṣmaparva 6.30-31; Hindi translation by Pandeya, R.S. 1975: 2558).

Bhīṣmaparva (6.42-43) of *Mahābhārata*, describes Bindu-sarovara, as:

अस्त्युत्तरेण कैलासं मैनाकं पर्वतं प्रति।
हिरण्यश्रंषः सुमहान् दिव्यो मणिमयो गिरिः।। 42।।
तस्य पार्श्वे महद् दिव्यं शुभ्रं कांचनवालुकम्।
रम्यं बिन्दुसरो नाम यत्र राजा भगीरथः।। 43।।
द्रष्टुं भागीरथीं गंगामुवास बहुलाः समाः.... ।। 44।।

(North of Kailāśa is Maināka. Further north is the glorious and bright mountain Hiraṇyaśriṅga. Near it is located Bindu-sarovara, which is large, bright and divine and is adorned by golden sands. This is the place where king Bhagīratha stayed for many years to have glimpse of Gaṅgā) (Hindi translation by Pandeya, R.S. 1996: 2558).

Similar to *Rāmāyaṇa, Mahābhārata* also mentions division of Gaṅgā into seven streams from Bindu-sarovara (Bhīṣmaparva 6.30-31), but the name of the streams are a little different.

तत्र दिव्या त्रिपथगा प्रथमं तु प्रतिष्ठिता।
ब्रह्मलोकादपक्रान्ता सप्तधा प्रतिपद्यते।। 47।।
वस्वोकसारा नलिनी पावनी च सरस्वती।
जम्बूनदी च सीता च गंगा सिन्धुश्च सप्तमी।। 48।।....
दृश्यादृश्या च भवति तत्र तत्र सरस्वती।
एता दिव्याः सप्त गंगास्त्रिषु लोकेषु विश्रुताः।। 50।।

(After descending from heaven, the divine river Gaṅgā first settled in the Bindu-sarovara. From there she was divided into seven channels. These channels are named as—Vasvokasāra, Nalinī, Pāvanī, Saraswatī, Jambu-nadī, Sītā, Gaṅgā and Sindhu. Saraswatī, among these seven, is at places visible, but at some places is not visible. All these seven channels are famous in *Tri-loka*) (Hindi translation by Pandeya, R.S. 1996: 2559).

Similarly, reference of Kāśī occurs in *Mahābhārata*. Anuśāsanaparva of this text mentions a war between Harshvya, the king of Kāśī and the son of Vatsya, Vītahavya.

स वीतहव्यदायादैरागत्य पुरूषर्षभ।
गंगायमुनयोर्मध्ये संग्रामें विनिपातितः।। 11।।
दिवोदासस्तु..।
वाराणसीं महातेजा निर्ममे शक्रशासनसत्।। 16।।
गंगाया उत्तरे कूले वप्रान्ते राजसत्तम्।
गोमत्या दक्षिणे कूले शक्रस्येवामरावतीम्।। 18।।

(Sons of Vītahavya invaded the kingdom of Harshvya, and killed him between Gaṅgā and Yamunā. Grandson of Harshvya, Divodāsa, following the order of Indra, established the city of Varanasi. One boundary of this city touched the northern bank of Gaṅgā, while the other was extended up to the southern bank of Gomatī) (Hindi translation by Pandeya, R.S. 1996: 2578).

The above examples clearly indicate that, in the *Gaṅgā-avataraṇa* mythology of the epics Kāśī is not mentioned. This is in spite of the fact that at the time when *Rāmāyaṇa* and *Mahabhārata* were composed (*c.* 400 BCE – 400 CE), the history of the river Gaṅgā was in circulation among the masses and was absorbed in mythology. But, Kāśī perhaps had yet to achieve the status which was acquired by other religious settlements, like Kankhal and Prayag on the bank of Gaṅgā in our religious lore. (Vanaparva 85.88-97; 135.5-7; Anuśāsanaparva 26.26). In fact, Kāśī with its territorial specification of the epic times in every probability was just a political unit.

KĀŚĪ AND GAṄGĀ IN THE PURĀṆAS

Mythology of *Gaṅgā-avataraṇa* is elaborately described in the Pauranic stories. Gaṅgā is referred as *gama-gata*, implying its descent to earth in the chapter 28 of the *Varāha Purāṇa* (Kane, P.V. 1973: 589). *Matsya Purāṇa* (chapter 120.38-42), dated between 400 and 950 CE further elaborates that the Gaṅgā which descended from the heaven was divided into seven channels.

नलिनी, ह्लादिनी चैव पावनी चैव प्राच्यगा।
सीता चक्षुस्य, सिन्धुश्च विस्त्रस्ता वै प्रतीच्यगा।। 40।।
सप्तमी त्वनुगा तासां दक्षिणेन भगीरथम्।
तस्मात् भागीरथी सा वै प्रविष्टा दक्षिणोदधिं।। 41।।

One of the divided channels of Gaṅgā following Bhagīratha came to the plains (Vyas, S. 1957: 281-82). *Padma Purāṇa* (6 Uttarakhaṇḍa Chapter 240), *Brahmāṇḍa Purāṇa* (Shastri, J. 1973: 126-27) and *Brahmavaivarta Purāṇa* (Prākṛtakhaṇḍa chapter 10-12) (Jha, T. and B. Upadhayay. 1981), etc., also mention division of channel of the river Gaṅgā.

The story of Bhagīratha and Gaṅgā is also narrated in *Padma Purāṇa* (950–1400 CE). According to which after pleasing Śiva, Bhāgiratha could bring Gaṅgā from the hairlocks of the lord to the earth (Sriṣṭikhaṇḍa 111-112).

आनीयाराधितो नित्यं तपसा गजपुंगवः।
तेन भित्वा नगं वीर्यात्त्रिभिर्दन्तैः कृतं बिलम्।। 112।।
ततस्त्रिबिलगा यस्मात्त्रिस्त्रोता लोकविश्रुता।.... ।। 113।।

(After which Bhagīratha worshipped Gajapuṅgava. He, with his three tusks, made three holes in the Himalyas. These were named *tribaligā* and *tristrota*) (Vyas, S. 1957: 280, 607).

This reference corroborates the relationship of Gaṅgā and Bhagīratha which was established in epic mythology.

Elaboration of *Gaṅgā-avataraṇa*, in Purāṇas like *Brahma Purāṇa* (chapter 74.2-5), of 400-950 CE and *Padma Purāṇa* (chapter 240), of still later times—950–1400 CE. Now the event of release of Gaṅgā from the hair-lock of Śiva is said to be two times (Jha, T. 1993: 425; Vyas, S. 1957: 233-34). Once it was released by the Saint Gautama and the other time by the King Bhagīratha.

ततो भगीरथो राजा गौतमश्च महातपाः
तपसा पूजयित्वा मां गंगार्थं समयाचत।। 52।।....
गौतमेन समानीता गौतमी तेन कीर्त्तिता।
भागीरथीति विख्याता तेनराज्ञा वृता यत ।। 54।।

Even late to very late mythological stories of the Purāṇas mentioned above do not reveal close relationship of Gaṅgā with Kāśī, which is believed to be of great antiquity. However, *Matsya Purāṇa* (chapter 180-185), *Padma Purāṇa* (Sriṣṭikhaṇḍa), *Agni Purāṇa* (chapter 110), *Varāha Purāṇa*, Kāśīkhaṇḍa of *Skanda Purāṇa*, in the process of telling the significance of Kāśī, do mention close connection between, Kāśī, Gaṅgā and King Bhagīratha. Also in the list of many names of Kāśī like Ānandakānana, Avimukta, Varanasi, and names of tanks, ponds and rivers, probable picture of Kāśī, before advent of Gaṅgā, is suggestive. These narrations on one hand suggest a pre-Gaṅgā stage of Kāśī, which had plenty of waterbodies, on the other hand it also gives credit to Gaṅgā, whose flow raised importance of Kāśī.

KĀŚĪ OF PRE-GAṄGĀ STAGE

Pre-Gaṅgā stage of Kāśī, according to the mythology of *Matsya Purāṇa*, (chapter 182.7) is a dialogue between the Lord Śiva and his consort Pārvatī (Vyas, S. 1954: 537). When Pārvatī asked Śiva why he has left mountain Kailāśa, he replied:

वाराणस्यांनदीपुण्या सिद्धगंधर्वसेविता।
प्रविष्टा त्रिपथा गंगा तस्मिन्क्षेत्रेममप्रिये।। 7।।

(Oh dear ! Varanasi which is served by saints, *gandharvas*, and where Gaṅgā has come, that region is close to my heart).

In another reference of Siṣṭikhaṇda (14.188-189) of *Padma Purāṇa* (Vyas, S. 1957: 104) in order to free Rudra from killing of Brahmā, Brahmā tells him:

........पंचक्रोशप्रमाणेन क्षेत्रं दत्तं मया तव ।। 188।।
क्षेत्रमध्याद्यदागंगागमिष्यतिसरित्पतिम्।
तदासामहतीपुण्यापुरीरूद्रभविष्यति।। 189।।

(I give you area of five *kosa* parameters. When Gaṅgā will flow from the middle of this region, it will become very holy).

The above references clearly suggest for the existence of a pre-Gaṅgā stage in Kāśī in the memory of the people. Advent of Gaṅgā in Kāśī appears a very late event. As Kāśikhaṇḍa of *Skanda Purāṇa,* while describing various names of Kāśī, mentions narration of Śiva to his consort Pārvatī, about the significance of *Maṇikarṇikā*.

युगपच्च त्वया शक्त्या कंकालस्वरूपिणा।
मयाऽद्य पुरूषेणैतत्क्षेत्रं चापि विनिर्मितम्।। 24।।....

(*Yugapata* – together – I, the *ādi-puruṣa* (the first man) and you, the *śakti-rūpa* (personified form of power), have created this region).

For explaining the significance of Avimukta and Ānandakānana names of Kāśikhaṇḍa narrate the story to Sage Agastya and says:

....परमानन्दरूपाभ्यां परमानन्दरूपिणि।
पंचक्रोशपरीमाणे स्वपादतलनिर्मिते।। 26।।
मुने प्रलयकालेऽपि न तत्क्षेत्रं कदाचन।
विमुक्तं हि शिवाभ्यां यदविमुक्तं ततो विदुः।। 27।।
न यदा भूमिवलयं न यदाऽपां समुद्भवः।
तदा विहर्तुमीशेन क्षेत्रमेतद्विनिर्मितम्।। 28।।

(Pañcakrośa-parimāṇa is the region which was not abandoned by Śiva-Pārvatī even at the time of the *mahā-pralaya*. This is how it is called Avimukta. The lord had created this region for himself, when neither earth had downed, nor water was in existence) (Hindi translation by Tripathi, S. 1992: 9-10).

अस्यानन्दवनं नाम पुराऽकारि पिनाकिना।
क्षेत्रस्यानन्दहेतुत्वादविमुक्तमनन्तरम्

(This region gives similar pleasure, which is attained by attaining *mokśa*. This is why in the past it was named by the Pinākī (the Śiva) Ānandakānana, thereafter it was named Avimukta) (Hindi translation by Tripathi, S. 1992: 11).

There is also a story for the names of *Cakra-puṣkariṇī* and *Maṇikarṇikā* in the Kāśikhaṇḍa (26.37-53).

प्रागानन्दवने तत्र शिवयो रममाणयोः।
इच्छेत्यभूत् कलशज सृज्यः कोऽप्यपरः किल।। 37।।
सव्ये व्यापारयांचक्रे दृशमंगे सुधामुचम्।
ततः पुमानाविरासीदेकस्त्रैलोक्यसुन्दरः।। 43।।
ततो...महादेव उवाचेदं महाविष्णुर्भवाऽच्युत।। 48।।
खनित्वा तत्र चक्रेण रम्यां पुष्करिणीं हरिः।
निजांगस्वेदसन्दोहसलिलैस्तामपूरयत्।। 52।।
समाः सहस्त्रं पंचाशत्तप उग्रं चचार सः।
चक्रपुष्करिणीतीरे तत्र स्थाणुसमाकृतिः।। 53।।

(When living in Ānandakānana, Śiva desired to create another region like it. He glanced over his left body, after which a *triloka-sundara* (most beautiful in three worlds) man came to being. Then Mahādeva told him you are Viṣṇu. Harihara (Viṣṇu) dug at the same place a tank with his *Sudarśana-Cakra* (the wheel), and filled it with under water. At the side of this *Cakra-puṣkariṇī* (pond) he got seated and performed severe penance for fifty-thousand years) (Hindi translation by Tripathi, S. 1992: 11-15).

Śiva tells Viṣṇu:

चक्रपुष्करिणीतीर्थं पुराख्यातमिदं शुभम्।
त्वया चक्रेण खननाच्छंगचक्रगदाधर।। 64।।
मम कर्णात्पपातेयं यदा च मणिकर्णिका।
तदाप्रभृति लोकेऽत्र ख्याताऽस्तु मणिकर्णिका।। 65।।

(... This holy pilgrimage is known *Cakra-puṣkariṇī*, because it was dug by your *Sudarśana-Cakra*. But, since *Maṇikarṇikā* (the gem of my earring) has fallen here, its *Maṇikarṇikā* name shall be famous among folks now. Viṣṇu asked for another blessing).

काशतेऽत्र यतो ज्योतिस्तदनाख्येयमीश्वरः।
अतो नामाऽपरं चास्तु काशीति प्रथितं विभो।। 67।।....

(Since this place receives the supreme light of the jewel, it be also named as Kāśī) (Tripathi. S. 1992: 18).

Somewhat similar description is available in *Śiva Purāṇa* (Mathura Prasad 1989: 125-132).

Pre-Gaṅgā stage of Kāśī appears to be of very long duration. It may be noted that Bhagīratha has been identified in mythology as responsible for directing the flow of the river Gaṅgā in the plains, and a pre-non-Bhāgīrathī's stage has been mentioned. For instance, the description of Kāśikhaṇḍa (28.2), which is in the form of conversation between Śiva and Pārvatī, runs as follows:

तदा भगीरथो राजा क्व क्व भागीरथी तदा।
यदा विष्णुस्तपस्तेपे चक्रपुष्करिण्रीतटे।। 2।।

(When Viṣṇu was performing penance at the side of *Cakra-puṣkariṇī*, where was Bhagīratha, where was Bhāgīrathī) (Hindi translation by Tripathi S. 1992: 69).

It has also been mentioned distinctively in the medieval texts, (Kāśikhaṇḍa 52-69 and 70, that before Gaṅgā started flowing in Kāśī, the region was full of waterbodies. Descriptions of Dasāśvamedha and Rudra-sarovara are significant.

पुरा रूद्रसरो नाम तत्तीर्थं कलशोद्भव।
दशाश्वमेधिकं पश्चाज्जातं विधिपरिग्रहात्।। 69।।
स्वर्धुन्यथ ततः प्राप्ता भगीरथसमागमात्।
अतीवपुण्यवज्जातमतस्तत्तीर्थमुत्तमम्।। 70।।

(During the reign of the King Divodāsa, at the place in Varanasi city where Brahmā, performed Aśvamedha yajña, was known earlier as Rudra-sarovara. After the performance of *yajña* by Brahmā, it was named Dasāśvamedha. Later when the King Bhagīratha brought Gaṅgā at this place, it became very holy pilgrimage) (Hindi translation by Tripathi, S. 1996: 34-35).

Description of five rivulets—Dharmanada, Dhūtapāpā, Kiraṇā, etc. occur in Kāśikhaṇḍa(59.19-115), before the advent of Gaṅgā in Kāśī, which became very holy after Gaṅgā came to this region. The description of Dharmanada of Kashipuri is as below:

.......जडोऽसि नितरां यस्माज्जलाधारो नदो भव।। 95।।....
अविमुक्ते महाक्षेत्रे ख्यातो धर्मनदो महान्।। 97।।

(Daughter of Vedaśirā, Dhootapāpā cursed Dharma to become *nada* (rivulet, which was located at Avimukta region and became famous as Dharmanada.)

Dhūtapāpā has been described as:

इतिशप्तस्तया सोऽथ तां शशाप क्रुधान्वितः।
कठोरहृदये त्वं तं शिला भव सुदुर्मते।। 96।।
....मा भैः पुत्रि करिष्यामि तव सर्वं शुभोदयम्।
तच्छापो नान्यथा भूयाच्चन्द्रकान्तशिला भव ।। 99।।
चन्द्रोदयमनुप्राप्य द्रवीभूततनंस्ततः।
धुनी भव सुते साध्वी धूतपापेति विश्रुता ।। 100।।

(The cursed Dharma also cursed her in anger and said, "O! perverted mind and heartless, you also be converted into stone." This curse was subdued by Sage Devaśirā, to be *Candra-śilā*, which will melt at the time of the rise of the moon, and shall be known as Dhūtapāpā) (Hindi translation by Tripathi, S. 1996: 100).

Similarly, for the origin of Kirṇā rivulet, Skanda says:

तत्र धर्मनदे तीर्थे धूतपापासमन्विते।
यदस न स्वर्धुनी तत्र तदा ब्रध्नस्तपो व्यधात्।। 106।।
....किरणेभ्यः प्रववृते महास्वेदोऽतिखेदतः।। 108।।
किरणेभ्यः प्रवृत्ता या महास्वेदस्य सन्ततिः।
ततः सा किरणा नाम जाता पुण्या तरंगिणी।। 109।।

(When Gaṅgā was not there, then at Dharmanada pilgrimage, which was given by Dhūtapāpā, Sun performed penance. As a result of labour, rays of Sun sweated. This formed a white channel and started flowing in the name of holy Kiraṇā River).

किरणा धूतपापे च तस्मिन् धर्मनदे शुभे।
स्त्रवन्त्यौ पापसंहत्र्यौ वाराणस्यां शुभद्रवे।। 113।।
ततो भागीरथी प्राप्ता तेन दैलिपिना सह।
भागीरथी समायाता यमुना च सरस्वती।। 114।।....
..अतः पंचनदं नाम तीर्थं त्रैलोक्यविश्रुतम्।.... ।। 116।।

(Thus, in the holy Dharmanada of Kāśī, both Kiraṇā and Dhūtapāpā rivers got merged. Thereafter, following the son of Dilip, Bhagīratha, river Bhāgirathī also reached there along with Yamunā and Saraswatī. It is due to this that *Pañcanad tirtha* is world famous) (Hindi translation by Tripathi, S. 1996: 172-189).

The above mythological stories demonstrate a pre-Gaṅgā stage of Kāśī region, which was though devoid of the main channel of the river Gaṅgā, it was full of many water saviors in the form of ponds and rivulets.

ADVENT OF GAṄGĀ IN KĀŚĪ REGION

The mythology of *Gaṅgā-avataraṇa* and Bhagīratha's credit to bring Gaṅgā even to Kāśī region is mentioned in Kāśikhaṇḍa (30.1-9).

त्रयाणामपि लोकानां हिताय महते नृपः।
समानैषीत्ततो गंगां यत्रासीन्मणिकर्णिका।। 3।।
आनन्दकाननं शम्भोश्चक्रपुष्करिणी हरेः।
परब्रह्मैकसुक्षेत्रं लीलामोक्षसमर्पकम्।। 4।।
प्रापयामास तां गंगां दैलिपिः पुरतश्चरन्।
निर्वाणकाशनाद्यत्र काशीति प्रथिता पुरी।। 5।।

अविमुक्तं महाक्षेत्रं न मुक्तं शम्भुना क्वचित्।
प्रागेव हि मुनेऽनर्घ्यं जात्यं जाम्बूनदं स्वयम्।। 6।।
पुनर्वारितरेणाऽपि हीरेण यदि संगतम्।
चक्रपुश्करिणीतीर्थं प्रागंव श्रेयसां पदम्।। 7।।
ततः श्रेष्ठतरं शम्भोर्मणिश्रवणभूषणात।
आनन्दकानने तस्मिन्नविमुक्ते शिवालये।। 8।।
प्रागेव मुक्तिः संसिद्धा गंगासंगात्ततोऽधिका।
यदा प्रभृति सा गंगा मणिकर्ण्यां समागता।। 9।।

(For the benefit of three worlds, this king brought Gaṅgā, where *Maṇikarṇikā* was located [3]. A glance on this gives *mokśa*, it is Ānandakānana of Lord Śambhu, *Cakra-puṣkariṇī* of Viṣṇu, and main region for the supreme Brahm [4]. Kāśī city which is known due to the light of Nirvāṇa, Dilipananda (son of Dilip) Bhagīratha led Gaṅgā to this place [5]. Avimukta region was valuable before it was left by Sage Mahādeva. When Gaṅgā came here it became valuable like diamond- studded gold. (What to say then) ... in the Ānandakānana and Avimukta region of Śiva's abode, which always was the donor of *mukti*, its value increased further due to the confluence of Gaṅgā with *Maṇikarṇikā*) (Hindi translation by Tripathi, S. 1992: 156-157).

The earlier description that Gaṅgā's, channel followed the path made by the chariot of Bhagīratha is also mentioned in Kāśikhaṇḍa (chapter 91) of *Skanda Purāṇa.*

यदा गंगा यमायाता भगीरथपुरस्कृता।
तदा गंगा परिष्टोतुं रविस्तत्रैव संस्थितः।। 102।।

(When Gaṅgā flows in the canal made by the chariot wheel of King Bhāgirathī, Sun-god comes there to praise Gaṅgā) (Hindi translation by Tripathi, S. 1996: 18).

Kedarnath Vyas has narrated an interesting story regarding *Gaṅgā-avataraṇa* in Kāśī region (*Kashikhanḍokta Pancakrośhatmaka Jyotirliṅga, Kāśhī Māhātamya* and *Kāśhī kā Prāceena Itihāsa*). According to which when Sadā-Śiva Bholenātha saw Gaṅgā entering in to Kāśī region with great velocity, he became worried about inhabitants of Kāśī. He then went at the boundary of Kāśī with his *triśūla* (trident), and waited for her. After some time Śiva saw Gaṅgā, he went forward and tied her in his trident, and said, "Gaṅge ! before entering my city, you must promise that you will always flow in Kāśī for your devotees. And the inhabitant of aquatics in your womb shall never bother the persons bathing". At the place where Śiva held Gaṅgā is known as Śultankeśwar, where a Śiva-liṅga is still found (Vyas, K. 1987: Gh).

GEOGRAPHY OF KĀŚĪ AND GAṄGĀ

Pauranic stories explain establishment of the channel of the river Gaṅgā and its flow to northern direction. Kāśikhaṇḍa (30.1-9) describes a mythology of *Bhaviṣya Purāṇa*.

कुरूक्षेत्रसमा गंगा यत्र कुत्रावगाहिता।
कुरूक्षेत्राद्दशगंणा यत्र विन्ध्येन संगता।।
ततः शतगुणा प्रोक्ता यत्र पश्चिमवाहिनी।
तस्मात्सहस्त्रगुणिता काश्यामुत्तरवाहिनी।।

(Bathing anywhere in Gaṅgā gives *puṇya* like bathing in Kurukshetra. Where it is joined by Vindhyachal, at that place the *puṇya* increases ten times more. Where it flows in western direction there, the *puṇya* increases hundred times, and in Kāśī where Gaṅgā is *uttaravāhinī* (flows in northern direction), the gain is thousand times) (Hindi translation by Tripathi, S. 1991: 43-44).

The above description mentions two major curves in the flow of the river Gaṅgā. The reason for the north directional flow of Gaṅgā in Kāśī region is believed to be the result of hitting its channel with Vindhyachal. But the question is whether Gaṅgā ever flows in western direction before entering Kāśī region?

The following dialogue of Brahmā with Śiva of *Padma Purāṇa* (Sriṣṭikhaṇḍa 14.88-89), is also significant to note:

....पंचक्रोशप्रमाणेनक्षेत्रं दत्तं मया तव।। 188।।
क्षेत्रमध्याद्यदागंगागमिष्यतिसरित्पतिम्।
तदासामहतीपुण्यापुरीरूद्रभविष्यति।। 189।।
पुण्याचोदङ्मुखीगंगाप्राचीचापिसरस्वती।
उदङ्मुखीयोजनेद्वेगच्छतेजान्हवीनदी।। 190।।

(The Pañcakrośa region which was given to Rudra by Brahmā, which is very holy city, as Gaṅgā flows from the middle of it. Up to two *yojanas* Gaṅgā flows in northerly direction, and in the east flows Saraswatī. Another two *yojanas* beyond this Gaṅgā is known as Jānhavī) (Hindi translation by Vyas, M. 1957: 104).

Numerous references for the northerly directional flow of Gaṅgā are found in Kāśikhaṇḍa, one of which is mentioned below.

कामप्रदानि तीर्थानि त्रैलोक्ये यानि कानिचित।
तानि सर्वाणि सेवते काश्यामुत्तरवाहिनीम्।। 23।।
स्व सिन्धुः सर्वतः पुण्या ब्रह्महत्यापहारिणी।
काश्यां विषेशते विष्णो यत्र चोत्तरवाहिनी।। 24।।

(All the pilgrimages of the three world utilise the northerly directional flowing Gaṅgā of Kāśī. Viṣṇu! though Gaṅgā everywhere is holy and is remover of sins, even then in Kāśī where it flows in northerly direction, it is of special value) (Hindi translation by Tripathi, S. 1992: 72-73).

DEDUCTIONS

The above-cited examples of mythological stories help one to formulate some generalizations with reference to Gaṅgā and Kāśī.

- The above account suggests that though the earliest reference of the river Gaṅgā occurs in the *Ṛgveda* (6.45.31, and 10.75.56), the mythology of *Gaṅgā-avataraṇa* was not formulated by this time. It appears that, during Early Vedic period (2500-2000 BCE), Gaṅgā was not of much significance.
- Association of Kāśī and Gaṅgā also does not occur in the Early Vedic period.
- Mythology of *Gaṅgā-avataraṇa* is also not the subject matter of Later Vedic texts. *Śatapatha Brāhmaṇa*, for example, appears to suggest that even up to 1000 BCE, it had not been formulated.
- But, reference of Gaṅgā does occur in the Later Vedic literature, the *Śatapatha Brāhmaṇa*.
- The above account further clarifies that the *Gaṅgā-avataraṇa* mythology is one of the very popular themes of the epics. The origin of the river in the mountains of Himalayas has been portrayed as an important event. According to the mythology, this event is full of obstructions, and the release of the stream was at wide time gaps. Pre-Gaṅgā and Gaṅgā stages in Himalayas can also be assumed by the narration of myth. But, Kāśī does not fair in the mythology of *Gaṅgā-avataraṇa* of the Epic period (*c*. 400 BCE–400 CE).
- It may further be noted that Kāśī is not mentioned as important pilgrimage in *Rāmāyaṇa* and *Mahābhārata*, though Gaṅgā was accepted as a very holy river, and some of the settlements, like Kankhal, Prayag,

etc. on its bank were mentioned as *tīrthas*. (Vanaparva 85.88-97; 135.5-7; Anuśāsanaparva. 26.26). In fact Kāśī, with its territorial specification, perhaps, was just a political unit, during Epic times.

- Purāṇas composed primarily between *c.* 400 and 1400 CE have two types of narrations of *Gaṅgā-avataraṇa*.
  1. The compositions of the earlier part of the date bracket suggested for the Purāṇas (400-700 CE), repeat the *Gaṅgā-avataraṇa* mythology of the epics. For example, according to *Brahma Purāṇa, Padma Purāṇa*, and *Brahmāṇḍa Purāṇa, Gaṅgā-avataraṇa* was the event of Himālaya. Gaṅgā brought to Kāśī by Bhagīratha is not mentioned in other texts.
  2. Those Purāṇas which have *Kāśī-Mahimā*, as a separate section, include in *Gaṅgā-avataraṇa* story that the Gaṅgā was brought to Kāśī by King Bhagīratha. The narration of Kāśikhaṇḍa (part of *Skanda Purāṇa*, composed between *c.* 700 and 1300 CE), is classical instance for the extension of this myth to the middle Gaṅgā plains.

It may, therefore, be summarised that the chronology of *Gaṅgā-avataraṇa* myth was initially related to the origin of this river in the mountains of Himalayas, where this event was important, but full of obstacles. The extension of this myth as to include Kāśī, was of a later date, when Kāśī gained the status of a holy place. In view of glorifying this religious centre, which had also become famous because of Śiva followers, religious significance of Gaṅgā could be infused through the expansion of *Gaṅgā-avataraṇa* myth. Together, Śiva-Kāśī-Gaṅgā, merged with each other in such a way as to boost the status of Kāśī and Gaṅgā, as most holy geographical units.

The above account further suggests that scrutiny of mythological stories like *Gaṅgā-avataraṇa* can help in understanding the process of formulation and elaboration or expansion of myths, both in time and space.

ENQUIRIES TO BE TESTED BY SCIENTIFIC METHODS

A number of enquiries come forth which, if tested by means of scientific studies, could be of much academic value.

River Gaṅgā is described in two ways. One in the form of a large water resource, Mahā-nadī, and the other as one stream, Bhāgīrathī-Gaṅgā. The former is mentioned as originating from the Himalayas, and having seven streams. The second, Bhāgīrathī-Gaṅgā, which was initially a tributary of the large Gaṅgā, came to drain the plains.

- Gaṅgā's obstruction to flow from Himalayas into the plains, forms the major theme of *Gaṅgā-avataraṇa* myth. It is said that Bhagīratha, when found that Gaṅgā is captured in the *Jaṭā-jūṭa* of Lord Śiva, which is like caves of the Himalayas, prayed Gajapuṅgava, the elephant who had three tusks. He created three holes in the Himalayas, through which the river water was released.
  It may be interesting to verify, if there was in the remote past a major geological obstruction which had blocked the flow of the river Gaṅgā in the Himalayas. And at some part, the water was released through three holes, which are of later date.
- The other noteworthy description of the descent of Gaṅgā in *Gaṅgā-avataraṇa* myth is that the river followed the grooves of the chariot of King Bhagīratha.
  The question is whether there was some palaeo-channel through which Gaṅgā started flowing in the plains?
- The narration of *Gaṅgā-avataraṇa* myth with reference to Kāśī mentions that Śiva stopped the flow of Gaṅgā, just before it was to reach Kāśī. He is said to hold the river on his trident.
  This description again is suggestive of some obstruction in the flow of the river before it reached Kāśī. Was it the rocky terrains of Chunar, which had formed some sort of obstruction in the remote past for Gaṅgā?
- Two points are mentioned in *Bhaviṣya Purāṇa*, which influenced the direction of Gaṅgā were Vindhyachal, from where it starts flowing westward, and Kāśī where it runs in northern direction.
  One wonders if these curvatures and directions of the flow of the channel of Gaṅgā, are due to some very special type of geomorphology? The flow in northern direction is very significant both in view of the mythology and geography, as it is just the opposite of the general flow, south-eastern direction, of the river Gaṅgā.
  Scientific studies, keeping in mind the above enquiries if designed, may help us to understand the ancient behaviour of the one of the largest water channels of India, and also elements and proportion of facts and reflection of religious mind to such myths as *Gaṅgā-avataraṇa*.

REFERENCES

Banerji, S.C., 1991, *Studies in the Mahāpurāṇas*, Punthi Pustak, Calcutta.

Eck, Diana L., 1983, *Banaras, The City of Light*, London.

Eggeling, J. (trans.), 1990, *The Śatapatha-Brāhmaṇa According to the Text of the Mādhyandina School*, Vol. V., Sacred Books of The East, (Reprint) Atlantic Publlishers and Distributors, New Delhi.

Hazra, R.C., 1987 (reprint), *Studies in the Purāṇic Records on Hindu Rites and Customs*, Motilal Banarsidass, Varanasi, First published in 1940, Dacca.

Jha, T., 1993, *Brahmpurāṇam* (Hindi Translation), Hindi Sahitya Sammelan, Prayag, Allahabad.

Jha, T. and B. Upadhyaya, 1981, *Brahmavaivartapurāṇam*, Pūrvabhāga (Brahmakhaṇḍa, Prakritikhaṇḍa, Gaṇapatikhaṇḍa), (Hindi Translation), Hindi Sahitya Smmelan, Prayaga, Allahabad.

Kane, P.V., 1973, *History of Dharmashastra, (Ancient and Medieval Religious and Civil Law)*, Vol. IV, Second Edition, Bhandarkar Oriental Research Institute, Poona.

Mathuraprasad, 1989, *Śivapurāṇ Bhāṣāṭīkā*, Vyas Prakashan, Varanasi.

Motichandra, 2003 (3rd edition), *Kāśī kā Itihāsa: Vaidic Kāla se Arvācīna Yug tak kā Rājnaitika-Sāmskritika Sarvekṣaṇa*, (In Hindi), Vishwavidyalaya Prakashana, Varanasi, First published in 1962.

Pande, G. C., 2001, *Vedic Samskriti* (in Hindi), Lokabharati, Allahabad.

Pandeya, R.S. (trans.), 1996 (Samvat 2053), *Mahābhārata (*Udyogparva and Bhīṣṭmaparva*)*, 6th Edition, Geeta Press, Gorakhpur.

Pandeya, R.S. (trans.), 1996, (Samvat 2053), *Mahābhārata (*Anuśāsanparva*)*, 6th Edition, Geeta Press, Gorakhpur.

Pandeya, R.S. (trans.), 1996, (Samvat 2053), *Śirimadvālmīkīy Rāmāyaṇ*, Part I (Bālakāṇḍa), Kiṣkindhākāṇḍa), Geeta Press, Gorakhpur.

Pant, P.C. and Renu Bala, 1993, 'Ṛgvedic Neolithism', *Bharati*, Bulletin of the Department of Ancient Indian History, Culture and Archaeology, Banaras Hindu University 19: 103-112.

Satvalekar, S. D., 1988 (trans.), *Ṛgveda kā Subodha Bhāśya*, Pardi, Balsad.

Sharma, S., 2008, *Ṛgveda*, Part 4, Sanskriti Sansthan, Bareli.

Shastri, J., 1973, *Śrī Vyās Maharṣiproktam Brahmāṇḍapurāṇm*, Motilal Banarasidass, Delhi.

Shukla, K.N., 1978, *Varanasi Vaibhava*, Bihar Rashtrabhasha Parishad, Patna.

Tripathi, K.(ed.), 1991, *Kāśikhaṇḍa* (Part I,) of Maharśi Vyāsa Gangānātha Jhā Granthamālā, Vol. 13, Sampurnanand Sanskrit Universiy, Varanasi.

Tripathi, K.(ed.), 1992, *Kāśikhaṇḍa* (Part II) of Maharśi Vyāsa Gangānātha Jhā Granthamālā, Vol. 13, Sampurnanand Sanskrit Universiy, Varanasi.

Tripathi, K.(ed.), 1996, *Kāśikhaṇḍa* (Part III) of Maharśi Vyāsa Gangānātha Jhā Granthamālā, Vol. 13, Sampurnanand Sanskrit Universiy, Varanasi.

Vyas, K., 1987, *Pañch Krośātmak Jyotirliṇga Kāśī Māhātmya evam Kāśī kā Prācīn Itihāsa*, (In Hindi), Jyotiprakash Press, Varanasi.

Vyas, S.K., 1954, Matsy*apurāṇam*, Vol 1, Claiva Road, Calcutta.

Vyas, S.K., 1957, *Padmapurāṇam, (Sriṣṭikhaṇḍa)*, Vol 1, 1st edition, Claiva Road, Calcutta.

Vyas, S.K., 1959, *Padmapurāṇam, (Uttrārdha)*, Vol 5, 1st edition, Claiva Road, Calcutta.

Winternitz, Maurice, 1987 (reprint), *A History of Indian Literature*, Vol. I, Introduction, Vedas, Epics, Puranas and Tantras, Motilal Banarasidass, Delhi, A new authoritative translation from original German by V. Srinivasa Sarma.

10

Varanasi: Origin and Growth from a Geomorphic Perspective

K.N. Prudhvi Raju and Manish Kumar Pandey

There are very many eulogies by many from outside and within on Varanasi and that of Mark Twain—"Banaras (Varanasi) is older than history, older than tradition, older even than legend and looks twice as old as all of them put together"—sums them up all in a nutshell. Now, nobody should mind the claim that when Rome was being built Varanasi was already an old city, a flourishing centre of religion, culture, philosophy, trade and learning. Cultures have come and gone, cities were built and buried; but, Varanasi is ageless in its existence, continues to exist and would exist into eternity!!

In this write-up, an attempt has been made to basically explain why the urban pattern of Varanasi city is what it is *vis-à-vis* the geomorphic surface/feature on which it started and grew and also to explain the site and situation of Varanasi and the wanderings of the river Ganga east and west of the present-day channel. As the study deals essentially with the older part of Varanasi city, here follows a brief exposition on the possible causes for the general pattern of old parts of our old cities.

PATTERN OF OUR OLD CITIES AT A GLANCE

In the context of Varanasi, the oldest 'living' city, let us just have a glimpse of our old cities in general most of which are older than the oldest new cities anywhere. 'The old city is chaos'. Such a conclusion, no doubt, based on facts, is quite common which shows the old city as either unplanned or ill-planned. The problem starts with winding, narrow roads and the narrower lanes and by-lanes and very little 'elbow space' between one house and another and the resultant congestion. Hence, the more fortunate keep out of the old city which is inhabited by the less fortunate. Whenever there is trouble there (in the older parts of our old cities), the sentinels of law and order fail to grapple with the situation and offer its 'haphazardness' as an excuse. An erudite friend of mine made a few indignant remarks on the 'hell of an old city' and paid rich tributes to the British for their architectural marvels in the form of a few beautiful sections in some of our cities.

Many of our large cities, particularly those with historical background, present 'dual-morphology' with an old city and a new city. These sections are often called as 'pre-modern' and 'modern' respectively. One of the factors which give a city its morphology or pattern is the road network. Road network in turn is influenced by topography. The old city is characterised, most usually, by a closely developed maze of tortuous, narrow roads and narrower lanes and by-lanes. Varanasi especially is popular for its narrow serpentine lanes and by-lanes.

Many specialists of different disciplines studied the origin, growth, functions, changes and decay, of the ancient cities in order to understand the 'causes'. When one tries to look into the origin, growth, functions, changes of a city a question like this framed by Irwin and Smith (1980; p.136) would arise "What was their structure that made possible their performance or how were they organised internally and externally for their peculiar role?" But on the old cities which are still brimming with life, the specialists tried to perceive the brawn and brain of our ancestors who built them, arrived at a few inferences and conjectures for probing history is like feeling something in darkness and trying to make out what is it that is felt.

Coming to the context of our country, history is witness, no other land attracted as many aggressions and invasions as India. At the same time, history is replete with many instances of internal wars from within and external aggressions from outside. So, the natural instinct and priority of and for defence and security of habitations and settlements stem from this fact. Hence, enemy invasions and siege mentality naturally affected the pattern of most of our historical cities. Of course, some of our old historical cities had political and strategic locations.

The reasoning behind the winding and serpentine roads could be that the enemy doesn't have easy access for 'frontal' attack. The curvatures provide a good shadow for surprise attacks. Unlike the modern warfare, wars in the past were face-to-face and hand-to-hand affairs. Now these very narrow roads baffle the police in tackling the clashes which erupt quite often. At the same time the anti-social elements use the lanes and by-lanes effectively to go on with their 'business.'

Topography is one of the decisive controlling factors which determine not only the dimensions of the road but also the overall pattern of the road network. But wherever the topography is absolutely uniform and levelled, it is possible and most logical to lay and expect a geometric alignment of roads. Instances are galore in India where, though the topography is favourable, the road network is extremely curved and narrow. The old parts of the cities like Agra, Delhi, Lucknow, Ujjain and Hyderabad, the inverted 'S'-shaped passage through the outer wall like the one at Golconda fort in Hyderabad, testifies as to why the road network of our old cities is what it is. But a few old cities which have come down through historic times have well-laid geometric road network—like the temple city of Madurai and Jaipur; and, there were different influences and reasons for this.

The old sections of our cities which we now ignorantly describe as chaotic were once the best (Schenk, 2004). They were, in fact, very well planned to the needs of the people, then to wage war and offer defence effectively. The road network of our old cities and in most of the countryside which shows the same serpentine shape owes it to the efforts of our predecessors, most of which were later linked and surfaced by the Muslims and the British respectively, of course, quite for another reason.

VARANASI: GENERIC AND ETYMOLOGICAL CONNOTATIONS AND IMPLICATIONS OF THE WORD

With the background presented above, let us look at the origin and growth of Varanasi as a city. Varanasi as an old city fits into each and everything that is stated above and related to many other old cities of India. But there is something more to Varanasi than what meets the mind—the explanations mentioned above—in terms of the relationship between its origin and growth *vis-à-vis* the natural land surface on which it started, grew, continued to flourish and still flourishing as the oldest living city in the world.

The tree-dwelling humans when they came down onto the plains within the river valleys, one over-arching criteria for building their dwellings is 'the highest possible ground' with seasonally/annually flooded lower floodplain around it for filling their granaries and the nearest possible perpetual water source. So, there is geographical implication in

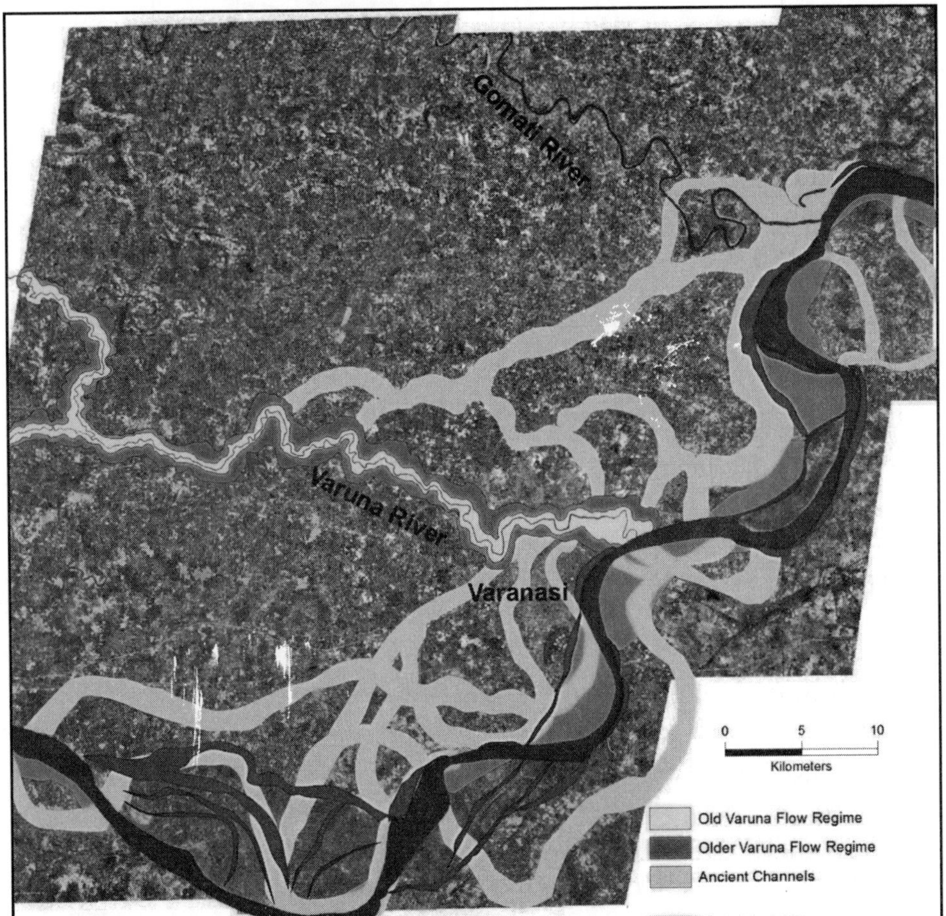

Fig. 10.1. Satellite image (IRS-P6 LISS IV 2006) of 5.8m resolution of Varanasi and its surroundings in the background with various geomorphic features and Varuna River regimes.

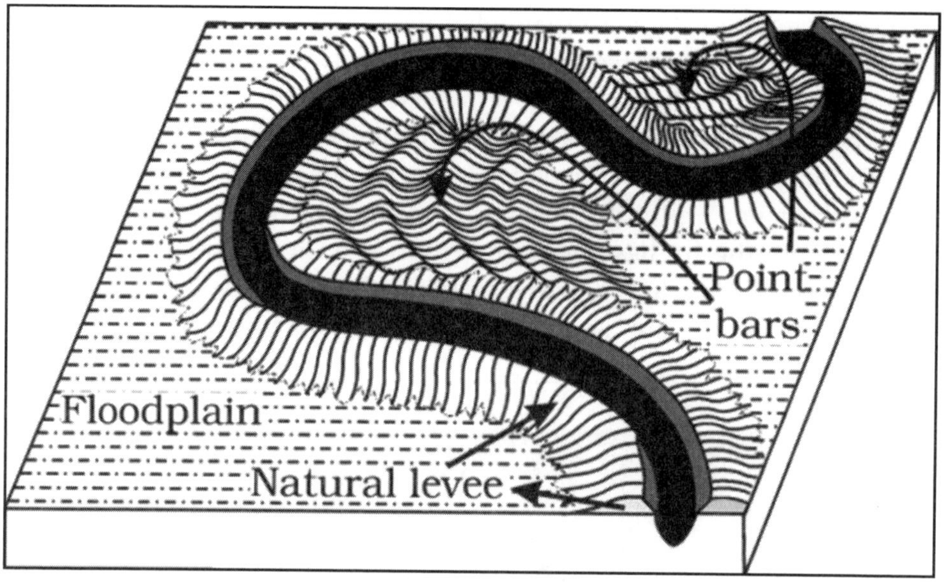

Fig. 10.2. A schematic diagram showing a meander loop in a floodplain with natural levee and point bars

the history of human civilisation and plains within the river valleys have given a direction to humans towards the so-called 'civilisation.' The vast floodplains of Sindhu and Ganga rivers in the Indian sub-continent are known to have many such human habitations of historical significance especially situated over the riverbanks. Varanasi (approximately centred at 83° 0′ 30″ E and 25° 18′ 30") is one such city on the bank of river Ganga. Etymologically and also speaking in generic sense, there can be many habitations by name Varanasi, for the word Varanasi means 'situated on the bank of Ganga'. Varuna (means the daughter of Varuna, the rain god) is another name for river Ganga. Quite surprisingly there is another river by name Varuna (though presently as a minor one compared to the present river Ganga), joining at the north eastern limit of Varanasi city. There are evidences of this river (Varuna) to be a large river (Fig. 10.1) and there are plenty of references to river Varuna (may be referring to Ganga or may be referring to the present river Varuna) and many cities on its banks, in Jataka (connected to various incarnations of Buddha) tales (Mukherjee, 1969). Of course, there is reference to the river Ganga—"when Buddha was walking along the river Ganga in Ayodhya" (Kashyap, 1959), and such references could be an indication that the river that was flowing through Ayodhya was probably called Ganga or may be, the river Ganga flowing through Ayodhya gradually shifted to its present location/course. Further, may be in the past, the Ganga was called by the name Varuna and vice versa. Both these names 'Ganga' and 'Varuna' are generic and any river can be called Ganga (means, water, from the sky to the earth) and Varuna, for both these names are connected with water. Similar is the case with the name 'Saraswati' which means, 'holder of sweet water'; in other words, 'the daughter of the seas'. This name 'Saraswati' too has a generic connotation related to water and that is exactly the reason why, there are many small rivers and streams in many parts of present-day India named Ganga, Varuna and Saraswati. So, going by generic sense, as long as water is there flowing as rivers and streams, there is a 'Ganga' a 'Varuna' a 'Saraswati' and so on and there can be a Varanasi on the bank of any river. This way, Varanasi is forever. And, by the way, settlement on the bank of an ever-flowing river, is considered as the ideal one and the best to live in.

THE PAST AND PRESENT ON THE LOCATION OF VARANASI

Varanasi, the absolute approximate location of which is given above, is situated on the left bank of river Ganga over a prominent natural levee. Normally, in the case of large rivers, when their waters overflow the banks (unable to flow through the existing dimensions of the valley), the coarsest load within the waters immediately get deposited over top margin of the bank because of deceleration of flow and, gradually with flood waters moving away farther from the bank, there is gradual deposition of coarser fractions finally thinning out to the finest fractions (clay) within the flood basin (Fig. 10.2). This process of flood deposits builds up what is called 'a natural levee' making up a prominent ridge-like bank of coarse deposits with good sorting sloping gently away from the riverbank. Such features can be found on both the banks along even straight river courses. Normally, within the alluvial floodplains, large rivers very rarely flow through straight courses greater than a distance ten times more than the width of their valleys, and, quite often develop meanders/loops (Fig. 10.3) because of fluid (water) dynamics influenced by 'corialis effect' caused due to rotation of spherical earth. Meandering courses of rivers and streams are more common in the alluvial floodplains than long and straight courses. And, in the case of meanders, the natural levees are built up on the concave/cut-off banks and point bars/deposits are accumulated on the

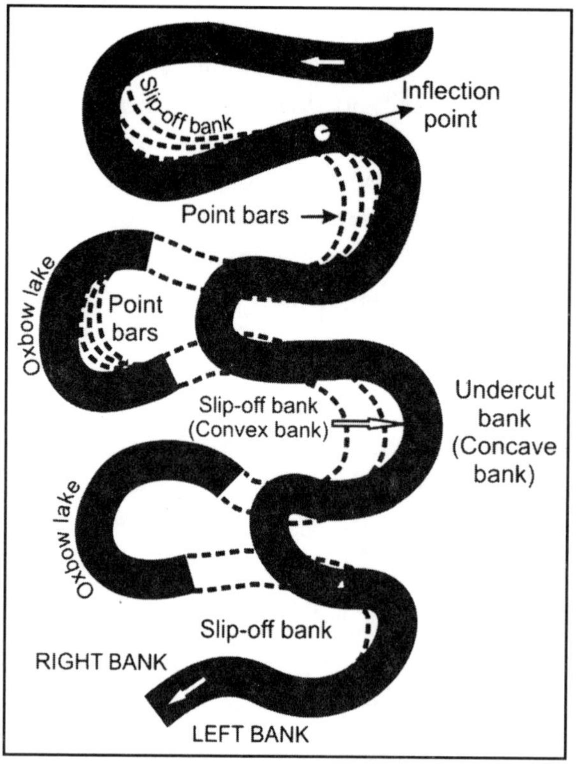

Fig. 10.3 A schematic diagram showing meander loops and other associated features

convex/slip-off banks (Fig. 10.3). In a natural environment, meanders are not normally permanent and continue to develop into deep loops by lateral migration due to erosion of the concave bank and simultaneous migration of convex bank in the same direction and by almost the same amount because of deposition of a series of point bars/deposits. That means, the general width of the channel from bank to bank would be the same because of simultaneous erosion and deposition in same amounts (Paola, 2004). So, when meander loops shift laterally, there can be a series of point bars or point bar deposits on the convex side of the bank and a natural levee on the concave bank. In fact, the concave bank shifts at the expense of natural levee and presence and prominence of natural levee depends upon frequency of flooding of water above the bank. On such a prominent natural levee of the concave (left) bank of a meander of the river Ganga, is situated the city eternal, Varanasi (Fig. 10.1). Normally the concave bank in a meander loop is steep and quite often presents itself with a vertical face (in the form of an escarpment) and the convex bank is gentle. An alignment of such long escarpments of concave banks of three or more meander loops of any river is not uncommon and is sometimes mistaken to be the result of faulting. This is because the concave bank is erosional and the convex bank is depositional in nature (Paola, op. cit.). The concave bank can cave in and cause destruction and the convex bank progrades by continuous deposition preventing easy accessibility to water. Normally, large habitations/cities develop only along the concave bank but not along convex bank in spite of the fact, the concave bank is vulnerable to erosion. On the concave bank, the water of the channel flows always touching the lower part of the bank/natural levee and hence water is accessible easily. On the other hand, the water along the convex bank recedes (away from the settlement after once it is established) along with the progradation of the bank due to continuous depositional process. This is exactly the reason why large habitations develop over the natural levees along the concave bank. This is almost the case in case of all large habitations along meandering rivers. Of course, it is a different matter, once after a large habitation develops along a concave bank, if the river channel shifts because of cut-off, the habitations end up on the side of convex banks. That means the early habitations like Varanasi developed along the concave banks with a clear understanding of river channel processes.

CHANNEL DYNAMICS OF RIVER GANGA WITH RESPECT TO VARANASI

In the case of the loop of river Ganga here at Varanasi, the recent (Holocene) point bars up to the present convex bank cover a distance of about 5 km. This doesn't mean, with the concave bank where it is now, the right bank margin was once at the farthest point bar in the east with the riverbed spanned about 6.5 km of distance (from the present left bank to the farthest point bar). What it actually means is, when the right bank was at its farthest in the east (marked by the presence of a point bar), the right bank was not definitely at its present location but rather at a distance much further towards east keeping the width of the valley almost the same or less than its present width. That means the history of habitation of Varanasi at its current location started may be in the recent times during may be the last quarter of the Holocene but not definitely earlier than that. But, if at all, going by the explanation of maintenance of channel width given above, Varanasi city was there on the older left bank that is expected towards east of the current left bank, it was washed out but the habitation continued on the shifting left bank (because of erosion) along with the shifting of right bank (because of deposition).

Also, there are evidences to show that the channel of the river Ganga here was once flowing, before it could establish its present course, a few km towards west of the present course. Evidences are indirect. At a depth of about 18-20m there is colluvial coarse sandy deposits (footslope deposits) exposed in the cliff of the right bank (Shukla, 2006). It is not too far-fetched to say that this colluvial coarse sandy deposit extended up to a little beyond the left bank. The presence of this colluvial horizon and river Ganga cutting through it is proof enough to show that the course of river Ganga was much towards west of the present-day course allowing the toe of the colluvial deposits from Vindhyan plateau (30-40 km east of Varanasi) to spread without any interruption. Of course, there are other evidences on the surface in the form of a series of ponds and impressions of old abandoned/buried channel courses. It is not unusual and in fact it is quite common for the rivers to wander hither and thither in the alluvial plains, more so, in the Indo-Gangetic plain with tremendous quantities of load coming down the Himalayas forming into gigantic alluvial fans with anastomotic drainage patterns because of frequent shifts (Singh et al., 2007) and also pushing the rivers flowing across in the plain along the ever prograding toe margins of the Himalayan alluvial fans, down towards south. The river Ganga flowing as the southern-most large river along the Gangetic plain is because of this southward rush and push by Himalayan sediments. The river Ganga couldn't be pushed further south than its present location because of (i) presence of Vindhyan outcrops and (ii) many large to medium rivers and streams dumping their load at the foot of the northern margin of the Vindhyan Plateau. So, it cannot be said that the river Ganga had been in its present channel ever since it came to its present location. Again, in the evolution of rivers, headward extension of rivers plays a major role in the lengthening of rivers by stream piracies. In the Gangetic plain, there are many rivers which gained waters of other rivers and many more lost their waters to other rivers because of 'stream piracy'. The present Varuna river could be one such example. At one point of time, may be, it lost its waters to some other river and is now flowing as a misfit stream in a broad valley (Fig. 10.1).

Coming to the river Ganga proper, it flows up to Chunar, located just east of Mirzapur town, in a general east direction and then turns towards somewhat north-eastern direction. This turning is due to its encounter with Vindhyan rock outcrops at Chunar and consequent deflection and also because of a gigantic Son alluvial fan together with the build-up of many medium-sized alluvial fans along the margin of Vindhyan Plateau (the river Ganga couldn't keep to its east-west alignment here). In fact, the deflection is towards exact north and it gradually veered towards north-east. When it flowed north from this point, the channel of

Ganga was much towards west of the present course. This is the point which influenced many a shift of Ganga Channel towards east and west of the present channel. There are many complex scars of shift immediately after this point. Legend has it that Varanasi went dry for a long time and King Bhagiratha wanted to purify the ashes (the remains after cremation) of his ancestors with waters so that their souls are liberated and obtain salvation. To achieve this, King Bhagiratha did *tapasya* (penance) for a long time to bring water of 'Ganga' to Varanasi and 'Ganga' came down at Varanasi at the request of Bhagiratha. The authors of this paper suspect

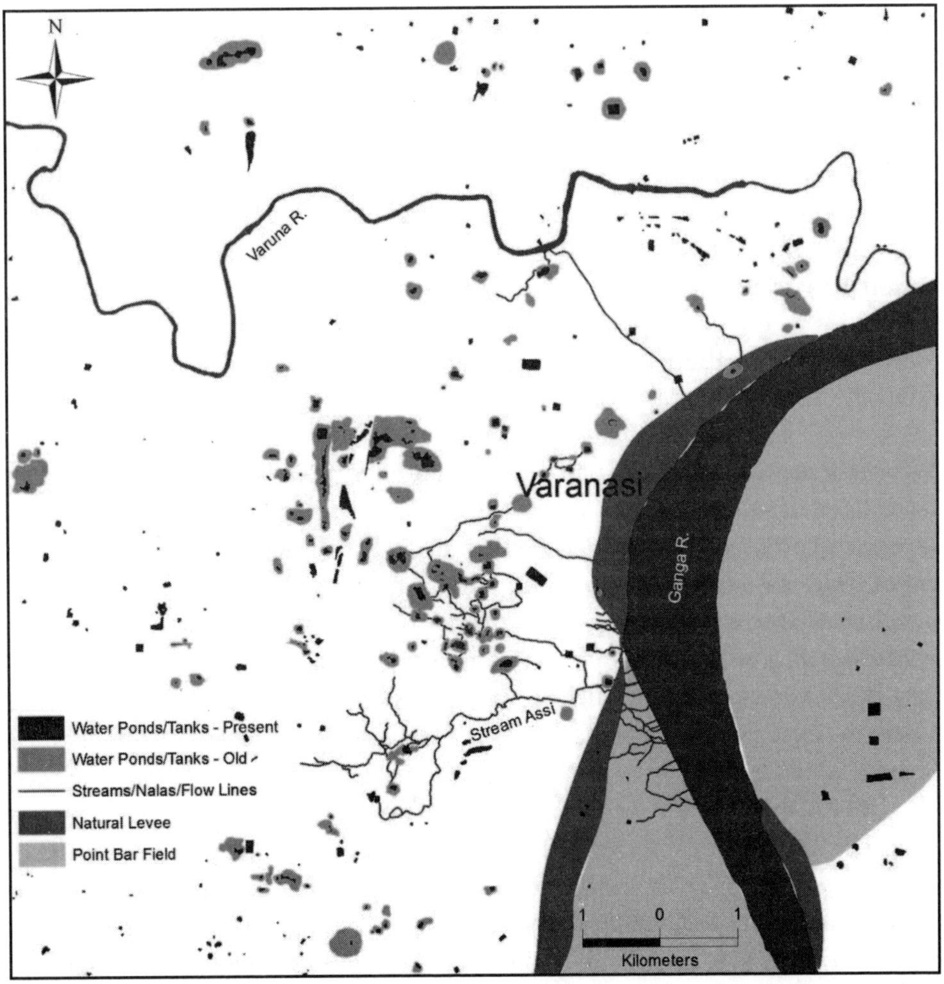

Fig. 10.4. A map of area around Varanasi city showing old and present regimes of water ponds/tanks and some other geomorphic features

that there was a gigantic human intervention (*Bhagiratha Prayas*—translated 'painstaking efforts of Bhagiratha, a person who happened to be a king') to divert the channel into one of the older (the present channel) channels of Ganga River. The implication of this suspicion is that, may be the present channel was one of the old channels that got buried or abandoned depriving the inhabitants of Varanasi not only of its waters but also in terms of ground water depletion in around the city and *Bhagiratha Prayas* (attempt by a sage-king by name Bhagiratha) is a gigantic human effort in bringing back the Ganga into this buried/abandoned channel. There are evidences in the form of preferred orientation of streams flowing down the Vindhyan Plateau towards east proving a point that the channel of the river Ganga continued its eastern journey in the past along the foot slopes of the Vindhyans. That means, there is predominantly three broad channel domains—one, west of the present channel and the oldest, second, the present channel possibly the second oldest and third, the present channel. There are evidences of the river Gomati's channel extending much towards east to join the river Ganga which was flowing much towards east of its present course. That is about the possible dynamics of the channel of river Ganga and its relation to the location of Varanasi city in the past and present.

URBAN PATTERN OF VARANASI VS GEOMORPHIC SURFACE

When there is a prominent natural levee, there can be many minor streams/flow lines on either side of it. Further, with a conspicuously high natural levee, a prominent flood basin behind it is also a natural occurrence. And, flood basin can develop into a large linear pond; or, otherwise, flood basin can break into a number of medium to small-sized ponds because of incoming streams debouching into the flood basin; and some of the streams can flow across the natural levee to debouch their waters into the river Ganga. As it is, Varanasi is known for many ponds and *nalas* (minor streams).

As for the development of the city of Varanasi , there was tremendous pressure on the land surface of the natural levee because of its elevation like a 'ridge' above the 'flood basin' on the west; there was also pressure of occupation of space closer to the riverbank in spite of possible destruction by erosion and caving. This desire to be near to water source emanates from the importance of water not only because it is important for life to sustain but also important from the point of view of daily prayers and rituals intimately connected with water. Water is the most precious and invaluable offering made to gods to propitiate them, for they do not have water though they have *amrit* (ambrosia) with them. It is this race that led to the complete cover-up of levee surface with very narrow lanes and by-lanes separating the houses. The houses occupied every yard of space leaving only the flow lines of water and minor streams which were in fact used as paths/tracks for movement. These flow lines have ultimately developed into brick-paved lanes and by-lanes of old city of Varanasi (developed over the natural levee or the so-called 'ridge'). Still these lanes and by-lanes carry storm water flow into the river Ganga. The north-south aligned stretch of present road leading to Assi Ghat used to carry water of Assi *nala* but has gradually become a road. The road leading to Dasaswamedh Ghat was once a deep stream/*nala* called Godaulia *nala* (extending from present Sigra to Dasaswamedh Ghat) which was filled to make it a road and the margins of the road were developed into shopping complexes and buildings (Kitts 1849). This is the reason why most of the *nalas*/streams and flowlines disappeared to become roads, lanes and bylanes. There are many examples all over Varanasi city where *nalas*/streams have gradually turned or made into roads both legally and illegally. In one way, this development, which appears to be unplanned or ill-planned, has done one good thing to the natural levee; it has stabilised from the onslaught of breaching by river waters during peak flows. The authors are of the opinion that Varanasi continued at its current location over the natural levee layer above layer of habitation and deposits from about 10m depth to the present surface level. There are evidences for existence of habitation at Ramnagar (Jayaswal 2006)—on the right bank of Ganga at the south-east corner of present Varanasi city, Rajghat—northeastern-most corner of present Varanasi city and Aktha (Jayaswal, 2009)—one of the settlements on the bank of the present river Varuna, on the north-west corner of Varanasi city. Urban elements have covered up the natural surface and hence it is very difficult, if not impossible, to trace the actual and natural surface features. An attempt is made here to study the patterns of various urban elements to understand the geomorphic characteristics of the natural surface. For example, the present-day ponds in the flood basin show a linear pattern (Fig. 10.4). Many more old ponds occupied or encroached upon by various urban elements show circular to sub-circular patterns of urban constructions presenting a contrast with the surrounding pattern. There are many ponds in a linear arrangement along the old course of river Varuna (along the northern part of Varanasi). There are also evidences to prove that river Varuna was once flowing down in a south-east direction and joining river Ganga around a general location where the stream Assi had its confluence with river Ganga. May be, this is the time around which Varanasi developed as a habitation on the bank of river Varuna (which ultimately abandoned its course because of intense fluvial dynamics to take a different course to debouch into the river Ganga towards north of present-day Varanasi city. The land of Varanasi is considered to be a piece of 'blessed land' because it was quite above normal flood levels. At some magnitude of flood, when everything else can be submerged in flood waters around Varanasi, the natural levee with a relative relief of 5-7 meters above the lowest level in the flood basin, the surface on which Varanasi has developed, can remain high and dry. This could be one of the reasons why it is treated as a 'blessed land'. Over the natural levee also, many local natural depressions were deepened and lined with steps; these ponds served as water source for religious as well as domestic purposes. There are evidences to show that there used to be stream inlets into all these ponds for filling up in addition to rainwater that used to collect into them from around and also natural stream outlets which used to carry away the excess water after the tanks are filled. Gradually, with the space getting filled by urban elements, these inlets and outlets got truncated from these ponds. The entire concave bank as it can be seen nowadays from its top margin to its lowest possible water level is lined up by heavy and large stones creating beautiful stone stairs running along almost 12 km of distance. These steps are fairly of recent origin from 18th century onwards laid out mostly by Maratha rulers and devotees (Altekar, 1937: 62). This single great effort of man has stopped further recession of this concave bank and damage to the habitation above it during the last 250-300 years.

CONCLUSIONS

Varanasi, the present-day city, started on the natural levee of the river Ganga. There were many flow lines/small streams/*nalas* on either side of this natural levee. Also there were many natural ponds on the leeward side of the levee within the flood basin. The natural levee was covered up by urban constructions and the flow lines were filled and were developed as roads/lanes and bylanes. The winding narrow road/lanes network owes its pattern to the patten and plan of flow lines/streams. The flow lines used to fill the many natural ponds and the ponds used to have outlets. Varuna river used to flow down southwards and used to meet the river Ganga where at present Assi stream/*nala* meets. In fact, Assi stream itself had changed its course in its lower reaches several times and had several confluence points with the river Ganga. Also, river Varuna used to have an extension of the channel much beyond the present Ganga and used to meet river Ganga when Ganga was flowing somewhat towards the east of its present course/channel over here. River Ganga coming down from the Himalayas after breaking into plains flows from general north towards general south. And, after a distance, it turns towards general east. Most of its general east-west alignment is dictated by the deposits of alluvial fans and other Himalayan rivers. The toe margin of the footslope colluvial deposits and alluvial fans along the Vindhyan Plateau margin extended much beyond the present channel/course of river Ganga. Gradually, the river Ganga established its channel over and across the Vindhyan colluvial deposits and alluvial fans. At one time when it encountered the Vindhyan rock outcrops at Chunar, the waters deflected towards general north-northeastern direction and the channel established its present course. This point of deflection caused many a shift of the Ganga channel from the present course towards east of the present course. That means, the present course during some period of time went dry and got silted up to a certain extent. At this time, there was Varanasi flourishing as a large habitation and it was deprived of its waters and went dry. To remedy this situation, there was a gigantic human effort which was recorded as *Bhagiratha Prayas* to bring Ganga back to Varanasi from its western or eastern course.

REFERENCES

Altekar, A.S., 1937, *History of Benares (From Earliest Times Down to 1937)*, The Culture Publication House, Banaras Hindu University, Varanasi, p. 62.

Jayaswal, V., and Manoj Kumar, 2006, 'Excavations at Ramnagar 2005-06: Discovery of Supporting Settlement of Ancient Varanasi', *Puratattva*, Vol. 36, pp. 85-92.

Jayaswal, V., 2009, *Ancient Varanasi: An Archaeological Perspective*, Aryan Books International, New Delhi, p. 232.

Kashyap, B.J. (ed.), (1959), 'Ekam samaye Bhagava ayujjhayam viharati gangaya nadiya tire' *Samyutta Nikaya* III: 358 (in: A Study of Ayodhya in Pali Literature,

Kumar Bimalendra, 1994, *'Mahabodhi', Journal of Maha Bodi Society of India* 102(1and2): 5-7).

Kitts, M., 1849, Memo on Godaulia Nala, Record Series of Collectorate Office, Varanasi, Vol. 44.

Mukherjee, A.B., 1969, 'Rural Settlements in the Jatakas', *Geographical Review of India,* Vol. 31, pp. 17-32.

Paola, C., 2004, 'Meandering', in *Encyclopaedia of Geomorphology,* by A.S. Goudie, Routledge, Taylor and Francis Group (eds.) Vol. 2, pp. 665-667.

Press, Irwin and M. Estellie Smith, 1980, *Urban Place and Process: Readings in the Anthropology of Cities,* MacMillan Press, p. 487.

Schenk, H., 1986, 'Residential Immobility in Urban India', *Geographical Review,* Vol. 76, no. 2, Thematic Issue: Asian Urbanization (April, 1986), pp. 184-194.

Shukla, U.K., 2006, 'Evidence for Palaeofloods at Ramnagar', *Jnana-Pravaha Bulletin* No. 9: 149-150.

Singh, M., I.B. Singh and G. Müller, 2007, 'Sediment Characteristics and Transportation Dynamics of the Ganga River', *Geomorphology* 8(1-2): 144-175.

Observations

11

Myths, Consciousness and Science of Signs

Gautam Chatterjee

While I was listening to Prof. P. Krishna's and Prof. Ramkrishnan's very significant deliberations on 'Do Indian Myths Have a Scientific Basis?', and 'Myths and Scietific Methods', I realised that some of my observations on the consciousnes and myths, a theme on which I am concentrating for quite some time, have relevance to their themes, which I propose to mention in brief under two heads—*Myth in Terms of Consciousness* and *Science of Signs.*

MYTH IN TERMS OF CONSCIOUSNESS

Consciousness has now become an umbrella word due to numerous views and interpretations of this term. I cite here two divergent views which enumerate its multifaceted essence and nature. Contribution to our culture, including myths, though is inherent in these explainations of consciousness, these provide opposite facies.

According to Western scholars, "Consciousness (is)...

1. Extended mind located somewhere in the brain,
2. Full of content,
3. Intentional,
4. Consciousness and knowledge are regarded as the same, and

5. No clear distinction between life and consciousness exists".

But, to Indian understanding "Consciousness (is) ...

1. Self-existent, self-luminous and self-dependent,
2. Contentless,
3. Non-intentional,
4. When combined with mind emerges knowledge (which is emergent phenomenon), and
5. has two faces—immanent and transcendent".

The immanent face of consciousness is always concealed from the immediate eyes which are conditioned to look at things empirically. To see through our senses is to perceive empirically. Matter or thing or object is always perceived empirically. Consciousness is inherent, concealed, thus, to be revealed. When it is revealed, one transcends the surface, the outward phenomenon of the thing is, therefore, observed. As one goes deeper and transcends in one's mind, it implies that one passes through many mental levels. These levels are constituted by things and thoughts emerging from things. The crust of the process is that the outside objects and icons are basically thoughts of inside (mind). Hence in the process of transcending, one moves towards higher state of mind, which is an aspiring mind. Inspiring mind is in fact the *chitta*, the mind aspiring for communion with the supreme. Thus, the transcendent face, which is also known as I-Consciousness or Absolute Consciousness, is the other face of consciousness.

Seers and sages practised to attain Absolute Consciousness with their aspiring minds. One can get a number of instances to suggest that in ancient period, in India, this state of consciousness was often attained, and communicated to general masses, who efforted to understand this phenomenon, the *chitta*. One is also aware that with a view to communicating this extraordinary experience and knowledge with the fellow seers, specific kind of languages—Natha-Siddha tradition (upside-down language), and twilight language (in Buddhist Tantrik tradition), were in practice. But, in order to communicate their experience and knowledge with laymen, seers maintained mental plane of the empirical beings. For this, they used the narrative and folk languages, which could be identified as mythology.

Since a story, an allegory or any content is weaved with language, similarly a myth is always composed of language—mythology. To me it appears that it was mythology in which language, seers used to narrate the wisdom of their transcendental experiences. It may also be added that all deities and actions symbolise specific connotations, which are hidden realities in the deeper levels of our mind. Revolving the stories around divine personalities helped conveying these experiences as divine messages, so that an aspirant of immanent plane could comprehend. Thus, to convey the truth or wisdom attained at transcendental level, seers used myths and mythological stories (language) in ancient India. One can well argue that it is for this very reason the origin of all the religious texts in India is owned by the 'divine'. As is the case with the accepted view that the origin of Vedas including the *Pancham Veda*, i.e. *Natyashastra*, is of divine origin. It is believed so, because the realization of their contents actually is from the transcendental level of consciousness of the seers. But, the texts were composed for the immanent level of consciousness for the benefit of the masses.

I would like to conclude by saying, that, the 'Consciousness' (transcendental) is the goal, when it is attained or realised, it is 'Science'.

SCIENCE OF SIGNS

Semiotics is a scientific study of signs. It includes Semantics and Pragmatics. Semantics determines relation between signs and its objects, while Pragmatics is the study of relation between signs and their effects. Another important branch of linguistics is hermeneutics. In ancient Greece, Hermeneutics were those who used to convey the messages of God, thus were regarded as messengers of God. In English literature of 19th and 20th centuries, hermeneutics meant the act of interpretation as to how to read an ancient exegesis or biblical text. This is now known as reception theory or reception aesthetics. Hermeneutics gives more emphasis on the act of reading the text in comparison to the ancient text or the author. The act of reading is a present act and not of the past or ancient times. Hermeneutics, thus, can be accepted as a scientific method to decode the hidden meaning of ancient texts or myths.

This method was introduced in the 19th century, and is applied as scientific method in modern times to the study of the texts and myths. But, its history is ancient, particularly in India. Ancient Indian hermeneutics is also different from the modern, as it never approaches a text from outside, which amounts to 'Mimansa', according to this concept. Indian hermeneutics accepts that a text or exegesis or myth consists of its own hermeneutics. For, it was the wisdom of ancient seers that they composed and compiled their sutras in such a way that only the deserved seekers of truth were able to comprehend their compositions. The encapsulated wisdom itself gives the way to enter into the new zone of understanding of the mythical language. It remains mystic until the seeker understands it thoroughly.

It is apparent that Absolute wisdom or to relish rapture of bliss through Yoga is difficult for a layman, but it is easy to understand the same through myths. It was for this reason that the ancient sages and mystiques introduced this scientific method called Indian hermeneutics, through which it was possible to understand and conceive internal wisdom in the form of myths, which are the external replica. The word 'Replica' is suggestive of the truth or the wisdom being always inherent in it.

It is, thus, possible to understand the myth of Dedulus or the myth of Raas, or the myth of Urvashi and heaven through Indian hermeneutics, scientifically. As it determines relationship between sign and its object and at the same time reveals relationship between sign and its effect.

REFERENCES

Baars, J. Bernard, 1997, *In the Theatre of Consciousness*, Oxford University Press, New York.

Chalmers, J. David., 1997, *Conscious Mind in Search of a Fundamental Theory*, Oxford University Press, New York.

Couzen-Hoy, David, 1981, *The Critical Circle*, University of California Press.

Ferguson, Sinclair B, J.I. David F. Wright, 1988, *New Dictionary of Theology*, Downers Grove I.ll: InterVarsity Press.

Grondin, Jean, 1994, *Introduction to Philosophical Hermeneutics*, Yale University Press, 21-22.

Life, Mind and Consciousness, Selected papers, Rama Krishna Mission Institute of Culture, Kolkata.

Understanding Consciousness, Recent Studies, Rama Krishna Mission Institute of Culture, Kolkata.

12

Myths and Science

S. C. Lakhotia

This interdisciplinary seminar on 'Myths and Scientific Studies' is very interesting and topical, especially in the context of the Banaras Hindu University, which provides enormous scope for such interdisciplinary discourses. The case studies presented in this session relate to Varanasi and provide a good beginning to the interdisciplinary dialogue. I would like to first make a few general remarks about my personal perceptions of myths/mythology and science.

As a biologist, I believe that a basic property of all living organisms, from simplest to the most complex one (including human) is to obtain information about their environment and modulate their biological activities accordingly. If the organism fails to respond appropriately and effectively, it suffers in diverse ways, including even the possibility of losing its life. Different organisms have different mechanisms to obtain the external information and process the same for its response. I think that the capacity to receive these sensory inputs and generate processed outputs can be collectively termed as 'consciousness'. Further, I believe that all of these are based on the basic laws that govern the properties of matter that constitutes the living as well as non-living entities.

The organism may acquire information about the external environment passively or may seek it actively. While the passive mode of acquisition of external information is present in all organisms, the more advanced ones have evolved a variety of sensory systems to actively seek this information and process the same in multiple ways to decide the response at the level of individual cell or a group of cells or at the level of the individual organism or even as a group of individuals. The human organism has very advanced faculty to acquire and process the information, thanks to the evolution of spoken and written languages. Evolution of a structured language has not only been a causal factor in the origin of man but has also been an essential requirement for the origin and evolution of human social structures. Language permits the information (raw as well as processed) to be available even to those individuals who are spatially and/or temporally separated from the initial event that led to acquisition and processing of the specific information.

The survival instinct is inherent in all organisms and is manifest in diverse ways. Man, with its highly evolved language and social structure, manifests the survival instinct in diversely complicated ways. It appears that fear of the unknown has increased as the intellectual faculties and social systems progressed and as the material possessions of individuals and societies improved. At the same time, in order to maintain the society, and therefore the individual, various codes of conduct (often termed 'religion') have evolved in different societies/cultures. I like to view the myths and mythological stories in context of the fear of the unknown and the diverse codes of conduct that have evolved in parallel with the evolution of different human societies/cultures.

Story-making and story-telling is part of the human nature. Stories can be based on real events and these form the basis of all history. Other stories are imaginatively created for amusement/entertainment and/or for conveying the dos and don'ts to the society in general. As time passes by, all stories undergo involuntary or voluntary changes/modifications. However, at a distant time it becomes very difficult to distinguish between stories based on real historical events and those that were more imaginative or purely a piece of literary writing (fiction). Human nature, more so in the Indian culture, to deify individuals of great accomplishments, taints even historical facts and, therefore, with passage of time such stories assume supernatural connotations and become part of mythology.

Societies with longer existence and intellectual development have a richer collection of myths and mythology. Consequently, the collection of myths and mythological stories in India is as diverse as its people. Mythological stories, as Prof. Krishna has clarified in his presentation, relate to supernatural and they become part of 'faith' or 'religion' (as usually practised in a narrow sense). Being part of 'faith', the society in general does not want these to be questioned. Science on the other hand rests primarily on questions. 'Faith' and the belief in 'supernatural' events seem to go in a vicious circle. We must appreciate that our understanding of matter, energy and the universe on one hand and the organization of living organisms on the other, remains very limited, notwithstanding the otherwise astounding all-round progress in science and technology. Consequently, there are many phenomena in the universe for which we do not have a 'rational' or 'scientific' explanation. However, that does not mean that these phenomena are forever beyond explanations. I am sure that what appears 'supernatural' today, would indeed become 'natural' as our quest for understanding the universe moves ahead in a stepwise manner. In reality, when we say that we have known something new, what it essentially means is that we have moved a step forward to know what we do not yet know. This permits more precise and informed questions to be asked as we move ahead.

Thus the apparent conflict between mythology and science finds it origin essentially in 'faith' versus enquiry. An understanding of the needs and approaches of each would actually help convert the conflict into a constructive dialogue. Viewed in this light, the discourses in this session appear to be in the right direction.

The case studies in this session related to the 'Jataka' stories and a few other mythological stories on one hand and geological/geographical observations on Varanasi and adjoining regions on the other. The objective of discussing these case studies is to find the underlying historical and/or 'scientific' bases of the stories. The 'Jataka' or the mythological stories are likely to have had bases in some real incidents/events. However, given the uncertainty of their actual temporal locations and the inevitable mutations that these stories would have suffered during their transmission from generation to generation, mostly through oral recitations, it is indeed very difficult to discern the real. Nevertheless, an unbiased analysis of the stories in the light of local customs, historical, geographical and geological background would indeed be rewarding. One of the essential basic steps in such analysis would be a reasonably precise determination of the temporal scale to which the events, in stories as well as in the geological/geographical facts, can be correlated. This time sequence seems to be incompletely determined at the present state of understanding. It is necessary that such analyses do not get afflicted by circular arguments so that a plausible hypothesis is accepted as fact and used to 'prove' the next set of plausible hypotheses. We should not try to 'prove the point' but start the analyses with a view to seeing if the proposed hypothesis can be proven wrong since the principle of falsification is the basic approach in Science. It is indeed to be hoped that the first steps taken during this meeting will continue to move in the right direction keeping the spirit of enquiry uppermost.

Index